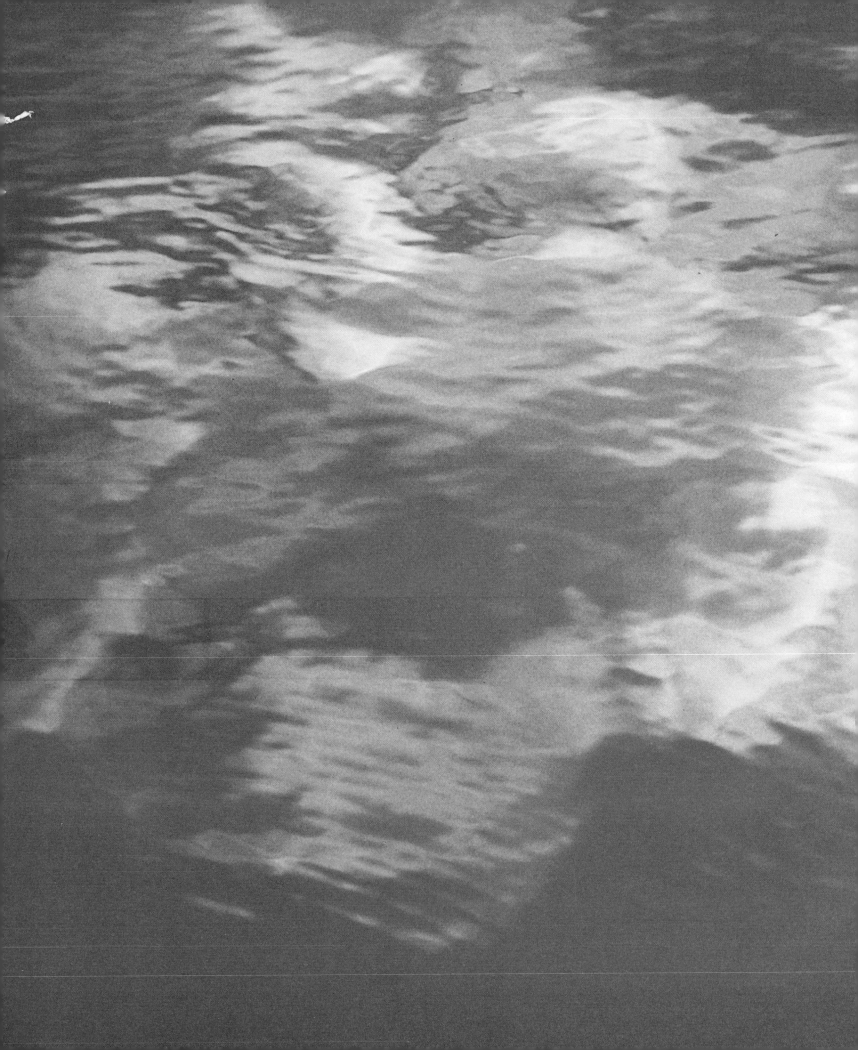

sally storey

lighting by design

PAVILION

TO CHRISTOPHER

First published in Great Britain in 2002 by
PAVILION BOOKS
64 Brewery Road
London N7 9NT

A member of **Chrysalis** Books plc

Text © Sally Storey 2002
Special photography © Luke White 2002
Design and layout © Pavilion Books 2002

Designed and Art Directed by Paul Welti
Publishing Director: Vivien James
Senior Editor: Zoe Antoniou

Printed and bound in Imago PTE Ltd, Singapore

ISBN 1 86205 528 9

2 4 6 8 10 9 7 5 3 1

This book can be ordered direct from the publisher. Please contact
the Marketing Department. But try your bookshop first.

**While every effort has been made to give advice on the safe use
of electricity, it is recommended that a qualified electrician is
consulted when installing light fittings. Regulations will vary
from country to country. Neither Publisher nor Author can
accept responsibility for any injury, loss or damage sustained
while undertaking activities mentioned in this book. With regard
to candles, never leave lit candles unattended.**

Author's acknowledgments

I am deeply grateful to everyone who allowed us to photograph
their houses and gardens without which the book would not have
been possible. I would also like to thank the designers with whom I
worked closely including Bartholemew Landscapes, Christopher
Bradley-Hole, Timothy Hatton Architecture, Alison Henry, Arabella
Lennox-Boyd, Mlinaric, Henry and Zervudachi, Karen Mulville, Rolfe
Judd and Taylor Howes Design Ltd.

On a more personal note, my special thanks go to Sarah Roberts for
managing the photographic shoots, Denny Hemming for her
inspirational editorial support, Elaine Parker without whom I simply
could not manage and Maz for looking after my children, Lucca,
Cazalla and Alexander, who did not see me for many evenings
during the photography.

contents

introduction

Light is among the richest experiences our senses have to offer and for sheer dynamic range, no other medium can match it. Every moment it floods our world with information and sensation, delineating everything we see. It affects mind, body and spirit alike. Yet although universally present, it is too often taken for granted, its potential scarcely tapped. By understanding how to manage this unique resource, our surroundings both inside and out can be transformed and our sense of well-being enhanced. The rewards can be spectacular.

Light can add a whole new dimension to interior design. Moving far beyond the purely practical, by using light imaginatively we can now create dynamic visual statements, enhance mood and atmosphere, alter colour and emphasize texture. When balanced with shadow, light adds subtlety and excitement, tranquillity and mystery. It can reveal unexpected aspects of an interior, introducing a sense of surprise, just as it can provoke and intrigue. A successful lighting scheme, with a variety of light levels balanced in harmony, can even make our living spaces more flexible, changing in an instant from light and functional to moody and atmospheric.

Until now, lighting has tended to be neglected in favour of colour and pattern, fabrics and wallpaper, the styling and arrangement of furniture. Lighting, however, is not merely an accessory to the overall scheme; instead it is a powerful tool. Where fabrics, wallpapers and furniture are solid and unchanging – until you decide to redecorate – interior lighting is a wonderfully versatile medium offering a kaleidoscope of effects from jewel-like precision to a subtle glow or soft overall wash of light. Through accentuating architectural features, altering dimensions and emphasizing height or breadth, light has almost become an architectural element in itself.

Innovative lighting designs, made possible by new technology and often drawing inspiration from the theatre, have now made light an essential ingredient in contemporary interiors. Where once Greek plays were lit by sun, moon or fire, stage lighting has achieved an unprecedented flexibility and subtlety, which we can adapt for our own environments. In the theatre, spotlights can be remotely controlled by dimmer switches, beams with hard or soft

The plain white walls of a courtyard become artworks at night, serving as 'screens' for projected images.

*Spiked miniature low-voltage
floodlights, camouflaged with a
green finish, throw a soft wash
of light on the planting in an
urban garden. A small concealed
spotlight, mounted on the
wooden fence, downlights the
lavender while nightlights
provide light on the side table.*

With the flick of a switch we can illuminate space but to bring a room to life with light is one of the most challenging design lessons to learn. The aim of *Lighting by Design* is to open your eyes to the phenomenon of light, to inspire you with the dazzling effects and the multiplicity of moods that a well-designed lighting scheme can achieve, and to help you to select the most appropriate forms of lighting for your own living rooms and living spaces.

Divided into three sections, the book begins by looking at the infinite variety of forms that natural light can take and how nature can provide inspiration for the artificial lighting schemes that we use in both our interiors and our outdoor spaces. Observing natural light from dawn to dusk is a wonderful way to learn how light behaves, whether it is drawing soft, dappled patterns or creating crisply defined shadows and infusing our surroundings with subtle colour. With a greater understanding of how natural light works outside, it can be introduced more effectively inside, enhancing space, revealing textures and saturating colour. It is also a powerful influence on the atmosphere of our interiors, making them welcoming, warm and energizing or

calm, contemplative oases in which the distractions of the outside world disappear.

Artificial light, by emulating the appeal of its natural counterpart, can transform the simplest interior into something sensational. Imagine layering light as you might layer the more tangible ingredients of a decorating scheme, starting with gentle washes of background light, then adding height and depth with directional lighting, and finally drama with focused beams of light and deep shadow. In this way, a stunning painting or decorative cornice can step into the limelight; subtle patterns can enliven surfaces and luminous colour can wash over walls. Having achieved the right balance of effects, the whole scene can be orchestrated by varying light levels to create exactly the mood you want, from warm and inviting to cool and sophisticated. A functional workspace by day can become a glamorous dining room by night – by means of light.

Lighting design is no longer limited to the interior but can transform the garden, too. Low-voltage technology has provided smaller, more creative lighting designs for gardens so that outdoor spaces can be enjoyed after dark

edges can flood a floor or pinpoint an object with great accuracy, attention can be drawn to significant events or the entrance of a new character can be dramatized. Fitted with colour filters and controlled by a lighting 'script', light is used to evoke a whole spectrum of moods throughout the performance, never intruding but rather enhancing the production by illuminating the players.

With the lighting effects now available, you can be your own stage director, transforming a room into a theatre of moody chiaroscuro or a luminous still life, bestowing star status on a fabulous display cabinet or focusing on a single vase and so flattering your home with light.

Natural light, entering a south-
facing bathroom window is
effectively diffused by a frosted
glass screen.

just as much as inside spaces, whether large or
small, in town or country. Entrances and exits,
and the paths that link inside to outside, can
introduce the lighting theme. Drama can be
created as effectively in the garden as in the
home with a statue or summerhouse becoming
the focus of attention, topiary thrown into
silhouette and trees uplit to reveal the canopy
above. Different moods can be created
according to whether you are dining al fresco
or taking an evening stroll through the garden,
while magical effects such as 'moonlight' and
water features sparkling with light can add a
touch of theatre for a special occasion.

Lighting by Design features interiors from the
simple to the sophisticated and embraces a
wide range of inspiring ideas. Lighting designs
are shown in urban spaces and country retreats,
penthouses and lofts as well as more traditional
homes, from London to Italy and the
Caribbean. The purpose of this book is to take
an imaginative and creative look at the
potential of light, and to reveal the effects it can
achieve, from a well-designed lighting scheme
for the kitchen or bathroom to atmospheric
effects for entertaining or relaxing, both inside
and out. Experiment and be bold with light.

1

the nature of light

A NEED FOR LIGHT IS UNIVERSAL AND EMBRACES ALL LIFE FORMS. WE ARE DRAWN TO LIGHT LIKE MOTHS TO A FLAME, REVITALIZED BY SUNNY DAYS, DOWNCAST BY GREY SKIES. LIGHT, AND OUR REVERENCE FOR IT, CONNECTS US TO ANCIENT CIVILIZATIONS, FROM THE AZTECS TO THE PHARAOHS, FOR WHOM THE SUN AS A LIGHT- AND LIFE-GIVING FORCE WAS SUPREME. ARTISTS, FROM IMPRESSIONISTS LIKE MONET TO MORE CONTEMPORARY PAINTERS LIKE HOCKNEY, HAVE BEEN INSPIRED BY THE QUALITY OF NATURAL LIGHT AND ITS EFFECT ON COLOUR. BUT ALL TOO OFTEN WE FAIL TO APPRECIATE ITS LIFE-ENHANCING QUALITIES BECAUSE LIGHT IS ALWAYS THERE.

WE CAN LEARN A GREAT DEAL BY OBSERVING LIGHT IN THE NATURAL WORLD AND ITS ROLE IN CREATING PATTERN, TEXTURE, COLOUR AND ATMOSPHERE. DURING THE COURSE OF A DAY, IT ASSUMES MYRIAD DIFFERENT FORMS: THE SOFT LIGHT OF EARLY MORNING, THE STRONG CONTRAST OF SHAFTS OF BRIGHT LIGHT AND SHARP SHADOWS AT MIDDAY, THE DAPPLED PATTERNS OF LATE AFTERNOON AND THE ROSY GLOW OF EVENING. LIGHT IS CONSTANTLY CHANGING, FROM MOMENT TO MOMENT AND FROM LATITUDE TO LATITUDE. NATURAL LIGHT, IN ALL ITS FORMS, CAN ENRICH OUR INTERIOR SPACES, TOO, MAKING THEM WARM AND WELCOMING OR COOL AND CONTEMPLATIVE. IT IS ALSO OUR ULTIMATE INSPIRATION WHEN IT COMES TO PLANNING ARTIFICIAL LIGHTING SCHEMES. WITH MODERN LIGHT SOURCES AND FITTINGS, WE CAN EMULATE THE INFINITE VARIETY AND CONTRAST OF NATURAL LIGHT IN OUR HOMES, FILTERING, DIRECTING AND MODULATING LIGHTING EFFECTS TO CREATE INTERIORS THAT WE CAN ENJOY EVERY DAY.

USING SHUTTERS TO CREATE
COOL INTERIORS – 30

BORROWING LIGHT IN
DARK PLACES – 36

DIFFUSING LIGHT WITH A
SIMPLE ROLLER BLIND –39

MANIPULATING LIGHT AND
SHADOW INSIDE – 43

HOW TO REDUCE GLARE FROM
SOUTH-FACING WINDOWS – 45

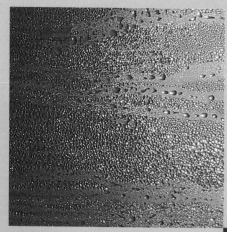

NATURAL LIGHT HAS A
GALAXY OF DIFFERENT
MOODS DEPENDING
UPON THE TIME OF DAY
AND THE SURFACE ON
WHICH IT FALLS. THE
STRONG SHADOWS OF
MIDDAY GIVE WAY TO THE
SOFTER PATTERNS OF
LATE AFTERNOON. MATT
WHITEWASHED WALLS
REFLECT A GENTLE LIGHT
WHILE POLISHED MARBLE
WILL BOUNCE LIGHT OFF
ITS SHINY SURFACE.

natural light

Natural light is responsible for everything we see in the world around us. It informs our perception of colour, it determines how we read shape and texture, and it animates our surroundings with patterns of light and shadow. Yet despite its importance light is often taken for granted. An increasingly urban lifestyle does not lend itself to making the most of daylight, and often many of our waking hours are spent indoors in semi-darkness. Only if we stand still and contemplate light as it changes throughout the day or from season to season – a pale mauve sunset on a stormy day or the luminous effect of light after snow – can we appreciate its power to transform our world, both outside and inside.

Without light we see nothing. When we look at an object, we are in fact interpreting the light that is reflected from it. Our eyes are continuously responding to light, changing, adapting and manipulating it, reducing or increasing contrast. Yet light is much more than simply what we see. It fundamentally affects how we feel and it influences our moods. Sunny, light-filled days result in many more happy, smiling faces, a sense of joy and well being, whereas rainy, overcast days tend to create depression, making us slower and less positive about life.

Our brains are so in tune with colour that we often memorize tones as we wish to see them, not noticing how changing light from dawn to dusk influences colour. The cool tones of dawn gradually change to a more golden cast. At midday colours appear more real and intense (unless bleached by the glare from an overhead sun), while dusk emphasizes the warmer tones of the colour spectrum. In northern latitudes, grey skies give a very blue cast of light, which makes colours seem softer and more muted, while Mediterranean light is much whiter, causing colours to appear stronger and more vibrant. Just watching the effect of light on colour at different times of day can help us to understand its subtleties.

Light is the connecting link between our sense of place, the local climate and our sense of time. Countries near the equator will tend to have full sun with dramatic changes between night and day. At other latitudes we experience more variable climatic conditions, and sunrise and sunset are events to be enjoyed as they light up the morning and evening sky. Wherever you are in the world, natural light has endless permutations, changing in intensity and tone throughout the day and altered by prevailing weather patterns, as well as by the seasons.

An overcast sky provides a flat, even, shadowless environment, very different from the effect of a clear sky with an overhead sun. While strong light can bleach out colour, it also creates dynamic shadows that move as the sun's position moves. Sometimes sharp, sometimes stretched out and elongated, they enrich surface texture wherever they strike. Patterns of light in nature, too, are mercurial. The lace-like filigree of sunlight on a forest floor that has been filtered through trees, or the rippling patterns of light that are reflected off moving water, are images that fluctuate constantly as trees move in the wind and as a river flows by.

The quality of natural light, and our perception of it, is the inspiration of American light sculptor James Turrell. In his installations, light becomes art. His 'skyspaces' are designed to frame planes of the open sky, encouraging us to think about what light is as well as what it can do. The cut-out space in a ceiling can portray a clear azure-blue sky or the shapes of passing clouds, or indeed it can be almost black in the guise of a night sky studded with stars. Viewers are encouraged to linger and experience the changing qualities of light, as it is only then that its subtleties can be fully appreciated and properly understood.

By observing natural light in this way we can start to recognize how light works: principles such as downlighting, where sunlight grazes a wall or illuminates foliage; backlighting, where a leaf is revealed in silhouette; crosslighting, where the surface texture of brickwork or gnarled wood is emphasized; and spotlighting, where a narrow shaft of light catches an object in its path. We become aware of the ability of shadows to conceal, and experience the drama of a rainbow as it paints a coloured arc across the sky. Each light effect has its own character and contributes to a harmonious balance.

By charting the passage of the sun during 24 hours, and noting where it rises and where it sets, we can discover the importance of orientation in our living spaces. Simply reorganizing the location of a room, say from east- to west-facing, can make best use of this wonderful natural resource.

Bright sunlight has an energy and warmth that we all respond to. When the sun is directly overhead, it is at its most powerful and the effects of light and shade are at their most dramatic. As sunlight strikes the whitewashed wall of a Caribbean villa, the beams of the open roof read in silhouette, creating a striking, graphic image (left). Passing through a round opening, light is focused on the adjacent wall as a bright, elliptical circle (right). Had the wall been directly opposite the light source, a perfect circle would have been formed. The power of the sun is indicated by the strength of the pattern, which in turn is governed by the depth of the surrounding shadow.

The quality of light on water is another source of pleasure. A clear blue sky, when reflected in a mirror-calm sea, will enhance the colour of both and make the view even more inviting. By contrast, the grey light of an overcast sky makes the sea seem darker and less welcoming. Frothing waves lend vitality by reflecting light, with sparkling intensity under an overhead sun at midday but with a more muted effect under cloudy skies.

Natural light enriches our perceptions of our surroundings. Our extensive vocabulary for describing light reflects the range of effects that it can achieve. We define a soft light variously as hazy or limpid, shimmering or luminous. Bright light can be dazzling or brilliant, sparkling or radiant. By the same token, light can be described as warm or cool. The forms that light takes are equally diverse, from moonbeams and halos to rays and streams. It is this sheer diversity of light in the outside world which, when brought inside, can transform our interiors, revitalizing and animating our living spaces and creating homes that are pleasurable, comfortable and welcoming.

In the bright light of a Caribbean morning, the surface of a whitewashed wall is broken by the dappled pattern of swaying palm trees. Countries close to the equator tend to have full sun with dramatic changes between night and day. Other latitudes experience more variation, with golden tones turning to a rosy hue as the sun sets. Afternoon sun bathes a Tuscan villa with a warm light (right), which accentuates the welcoming coolness of the dark interior.

We interpret ridges of sand by the fall of light and shade (below). If lit uniformly, the sand would appear almost flat, but when lit from an angle, it becomes three-dimensional. The soft curves and straight ridges are given greater emphasis, providing a subtle play of contrasts.

The play of light and shade changes constantly as the sun changes its position. Sometimes shadows are sharply delineated, sometimes soft-edged. A city sidewalk is decorated with the shadows of iron railings (left), which project a geometric pattern across the pavement, stronger at their base, then seemingly fading out.

The deep red of a plastered wall is
in contrast to the greenery of the
garden as well as a dramatic
backdrop to the shadows created by
nearby trees. Open leaf forms allow
more light to filter through,
resulting in more complex patterns.
The depth of the colours – red
wall patterned with black shadow
– adds to the richness of
the composition.

The patterns of natural light are easier to understand when viewed in isolation. The subject matter becomes abstracted and we focus solely on the forms of light and shade, which know no boundaries and embellish everything in their path, whether furrowed earth or rounded boulders.

Reflections play an important part in the role of natural light. They appear like images in a mirror when the water is still, but when rippled by a moving current or by the wind, they become a constantly changing pattern. An almost clear sky (left), softened by drifting clouds, is reflected in the water of a lake, intensifying its colour. Under the hazy conditions of a cloudy sky, reflections appear as abstract shapes or lines, like the brushstrokes of an Impressionist artist, while a bright sun will create sharply defined images (right).

NATURAL LIGHT,
WHETHER AS POOLS OF
WARM SUNSHINE OR
CORNERS OF COOL
SHADOW, ANIMATES OUR
INTERIORS. IT CAN
DEFINE SPACE BY
THROWING
ARCHITECTURAL
DETAILS INTO RELIEF.
SURFACES ARE
ENLIVENED WITH
PATTERNS OF LIGHT AND
SHADE, WHILE TEXTURES
REVEAL THEIR TRUE
QUALITY WHEN
HIGHLIGHTED BY
NATURAL LIGHT.

daylight inside buildings

The sheer vitality and variety of natural light and shade bring our living spaces to life. Light-filled rooms are instinctively welcoming and contribute to our sense of well-being and comfort. We take pleasure in the way natural light changes our environment throughout the course of a day, whether it is the midday sun slanting through half-closed venetian blinds or the dappled light of a shaded terrace. Always changing in intensity, light also introduces colour and tone, painting our walls shades of blue in the early morning and soft yellow in the late afternoon sun.

Light is a creator of infinite moods, and spaces can appear cold, claustrophobic, warm or energizing, depending on the quality of light they receive. The Koshimo House, designed by the Japanese architect Tadao Ando, shows how light can affect us. On the outside it appears to be a simple two-storey home, made from two concrete boxes that face each other. Inside, however, the play of light and shadow creates wonderful spaces of contemplation in which the outside world with all its distractions seems to disappear.

As well as influencing the atmosphere of our interiors and affecting our moods, light enhances space, which many of us now regard as the most precious element in our homes. It defines the spatial character of our rooms, throwing architectural details into relief, modelling form through contrasts of light and shade, tracing curves and delineating corners. Texture, too, is revealed by light, which emphasizes the material quality of different surfaces, from smooth stone and leather to crunchy linen and rough brickwork.

Changing fashions, local cultures and climate all affect our attitude to light. In Georgian England, for example, large elegant sash windows and domed skylights flooded interiors with natural light by day while thick window coverings reduced heat loss by night. Yet the following century saw light shut out, day and night, behind layers of heavy furnishings. Generally, however, in northern latitudes where overcast skies are prevalent, we try to maximize light with pale, airy colours and uncluttered window treatments, while minimizing heat loss. In warmer climates, with strong daylight and accompanying heat, small deep-set windows or openings reduce glare and heat gain while still illuminating internal spaces with shafts of intense light. Inner courtyards have larger windows, the light shaded by a loggia that reflects light indirectly inside. It is windows, with their interplay of shape and style, which help to articulate the design of a building.

Modern architects have all explored the inherent beauty of natural light in their buildings. But this is not a new phenomenon. A master in his manipulation of light was the architect Sir John Soane, whose ability to capture light from unexpected sources can be seen in his home and museum at Lincoln's Inn Fields, London. The spandrels of domes, window reveals, even the fillets between bookcases are decorated with mirrors, while ceilings are punctured with skylights encased in pale yellow glass to replicate sunlight. His ingenious use of glass block floors allowed light to pass from one storey to another, bringing light into the darkest spaces; even brass shelves and gilded frames were used to catch the light.

Our passion for space and for light-filled rooms is now fulfilled by totally glazed buildings, where even the structure itself is of glass, made possible by new engineering techniques. Norman Foster's Great Court at the British Museum in London, covered with a glass roof that resembles a giant spider's web, epitomizes new levels of lightness and transparency.

The luminous effects of natural light can be maximized in our own homes through a variety of simple strategies, starting with the orientation of space. It is worth spending time in each room assessing which direction it faces, how the light falls at different times of day,

whether it is predominantly light or dark. Many of us are surprisingly conventional when it comes to deciding on which room best suits which purpose. An upper floor might be more appropriate for a living area if the light is brighter by day, whereas a lower ground floor might be best for a bedroom, perhaps with windows onto a garden or terrace.

A fundamental change in the quantity of light a home receives may involve altering the basic framework: moving walls, creating new entrances, removing a portion of floor to create a double-height space or capping a side extension with a glazed roof. But there are smaller structural changes that can help to transform a home from top to bottom. An attic space used for storage can become a new bedroom or work space when fitted with a roof light or dormer window. A dark basement

The large plate-glass expanse of many contemporary buildings provides magnificent views as well as permitting maximum natural light with minimum heat gain, thanks to the heat-reflecting properties incorporated within the glazing. The resulting light-filled interiors are particularly welcome in northern latitudes. Light reflective surfaces, such as a leather floor, enhance the effect still further.

might benefit from making windows wider or deeper, and creating windows on two sides of a room, rather than one, will dramatically increase available light. The shape and size of your windows will affect the quality, as well as the quantity, of light they permit. Clerestory windows, for example, which are situated at a high level, create a gentle, soft light as daylight enters directly only when the sun is low.

Just as light can be brought into the heart of a home by means of improved external features, so internal decisions will help to amplify the effect. Glass in the form of walls, windows and doors will lighten any space, but it is especially welcome where there is no access to an outside area. Decorative finishes can also be light enhancing. Pale surfaces and colours are reflective, while dark materials absorb light. So daylight flooding onto a light-coloured floor – softly waxed boards or a cream wool rug – will be reflected up to the ceiling. Conversely, black slate will reflect very little light and your room will appear darker and the ceiling lower. One or two key objects with a shimmery finish, such as lacquerware, glazed ceramics or shot-silk cushions, will also help to catch the light while the judicious positioning of mirror glass, perhaps between a pair of sash windows or used

full height in alcoves, will throw natural light into the darkest of corners. Even reflective surfaces outside, such as paths, terraces and pools, can bounce light back inside. By selecting the right materials, living spaces can be aesthetically appealing and filled with light, too.

The desire to invite maximum natural light into our homes has consequently created the need to shield light or provide adequate screening to vary its intensity. Understanding the character of each light source, and knowing how to control it, is as important as discovering its benefits. The strength of light will vary depending on the angle of the sun and the point at which it enters a building. Light from above, such as a rooflight, especially when the sun is overhead, is more powerful than from other planes. Even in Northern Europe, west- or south-facing rooms will still require a degree of glare protection.

Screens have been used in warm climates for centuries, both for coolness and for privacy. With the *jali* screens of India and the *mashrabiya* screens of the Middle East, not only is light partially shielded, it also projects abstract patterns onto the walls and floors beyond, reflective of the complex designs found in

traditional carpets and mosaic floors. In Japan, screening has tended to be far simpler, relying on rice paper or parchment stretched across a wooden frame. Light entering a room through a *shoji* screen is softer and more diffuse compared to the dramatic contrasts of light, shadow and pattern that characterize its Indian and Islamic counterparts.

In the Mediterranean, a typical Tuscan farmhouse employs a double system of shutters, which admits a graduated light through the outer slats and full blackout with the addition of solid inner shutters. In northern latitudes, forms of screening include simple fabric blinds, which can roll up to create privacy and still admit light, as well as roll down to shield sun. Slatted blinds are adjusted according to the variable light levels, and curtains come in varying weights from translucent muslin to fully lined blackout. Advances in fabric technology have removed the need for the ubiquitous net curtain, providing countless semi-transparent materials that can be layered to achieve the same flexibility of light levels as a venetian blind or Mediterranean shutter. And stained glass has both filtered and coloured light for centuries, from the rose windows of Gothic cathedrals to contemporary glass panels.

Afternoon sunlight, pouring in through deep Georgian sash windows, creates regular, elongated shafts of light across a dining room. The shape of the windows is reflected off nearby surfaces, the crispness of the image dependent on the reflective qualities of that surface. Compare the image on the glass table with the softer reflection on the polished wood floor.

With the development of technology, fully glazed buildings are now common in hot as well as temperate climates, fitted with glass that can reflect or absorb both heat and light. Glazing units can have blinds incorporated into the fixture, while improved double-glazing and thermal properties in glass are a more energy-efficient solution than air-conditioning. Films can be applied to clear glass rooflights and conservatories to reflect light and reduce glare, while intelligent glass systems can turn glass from transparent to opaque at the flick of a switch.

Natural light spilling into a living space is a wonderful gift, especially once you have learned to cultivate its potential. Not only does it enhance our interiors, it also connects us to the outside world and lifts our spirits. Above all, it is a wonderful source of inspiration when devising our own lighting schemes. With the range of lighting designs now available, we can emulate the infinite variety and contrast of natural light in our homes.

Borrowed light from a small clerestory window (left) provides the solution to a dark bedroom, which looks onto a small courtyard that gets very little natural light (right). The small slotted top light allows light to flood in above the bedhead. Light then bounces off the receiving wall at a high level, providing soft reflected illumination and illustrating yet another means of using daylight. The shutters and French doors onto the courtyard are a visual play, as it is the top light that provides most of the natural light. Any dark basement room will benefit from structural use of borrowed light in this way, which can then be maximized by choosing a light colour scheme for walls and furnishings.

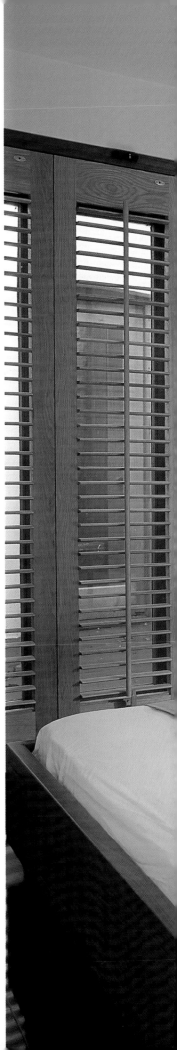

Light and glass are a magical combination. The transparent nature of glass is heightened by light until it assumes the merest outline of shape and form. As light passes through, most is refracted but some is lost through reflection, reappearing along the glass edge. The wonderful green rim that characterizes standard glass is accentuated by light in this way, often taking on an almost jewel-like quality.

The soft light from a north-facing kitchen window does not need much shielding, and the view of the terrace beyond can be enjoyed at all times of day. A polished granite work surface has high reflective values, echoing the lines of the window and dappled pattern as light filters through the bamboo outside.

An effective way of reducing glare from a south-facing window in the same kitchen is to diffuse the light through a simple white roller blind. The effect is softened, making the shadows far less strong, and with the glare reduced the impression is that of an evenly lit space.

Dark colours have a tendency to absorb the light. The gold brocade edging of black velvet curtains is the only element to reflect any available light. The effect is dramatic.

Evening sunlight in a bedroom projects the perfect shadow of an orchid onto cupboard doors of pale wood. The reflected lines of the window are more emphatic on a light surface than on dark.

Roof lights are just one means of bringing additional natural light into a space. An expansive roof light in a pitched ceiling (left) throws light onto the shutters, interlaced with the shadows of the roof trusses.

Strong horizontal banding across the back of a sofa (right) creates a wonderful pattern that appears and disappears as the sun changes position. Wooden shutters are a useful means of controlling light as they can be adjusted to suit the angle of the sun, either maximizing light or reducing it to full blackout.

A display of dried flowers (below) appears painted with strongly accentuated pattern, created by afternoon sunlight as it filters through the shutters of a living room. Fine stripes of shadow are caused when wooden slats are almost parallel to the sun's rays.

Sunlight can be filtered in varying degrees by layering fabric, from fine muslin to linen. The closer the weave and the heavier the fabric, the more effective the screen. Used as a flat panel at a window, muslin can diffuse light as efficiently as sandblasted glass; draped, it will intensify shadows. Using drapes to surround a bed can soften the effect still further. Besides screening views and cutting out glare, sheer fabrics are particularly useful for providing privacy.

Sunlight enters a bathroom through a deep sash window, the light reflecting off the enamel surface of the bath (above right). By night, when artificial light is in use, a dark silk blind is lowered for privacy, providing full black-out (below right).

2

section two

mood lighting in the home

LIGHT IS ONE OF THE MOST POWERFUL ELEMENTS OF INTERIOR DESIGN. THE MOST ORDINARY OF SPACES CAN BECOME EXTRAORDINARY, FULL OF DRAMA AND CONTRAST, WITH THE ADDED INGREDIENT OF LIGHT. IT CAN BE MANIPULATED TO DIM OR BRIGHTEN, TO OBSCURE OR HIGHLIGHT, OR TO CREATE PLAYS OF SHADOW AND COLOUR. LIGHT CAN TRANSFORM THE ATMOSPHERE OF A ROOM IN THE SAME WAY THAT THEATRE LIGHTING CAN ALTER A SCENE. A FEW WELL-PLACED FITTINGS IN A ROOM CAN CREATE EFFECTS THAT WOULD BE MUCH MORE COSTLY TO ACHIEVE USING SURFACE DECORATION ALONE. IT CAN EVEN BE USED TO ENHANCE SPATIAL PERSPECTIVES AND TO MAKE OUR INTERIORS MORE FLEXIBLE: ONE MOMENT A KITCHEN CAN BE LIGHT, BRIGHT AND FUNCTIONAL FOR COOKING AND THE NEXT, AN INTIMATE DINING ROOM – ALL AT THE FLICK OF A SWITCH.

LIGHT IS OFTEN THE ONE ASPECT OF DESIGN THAT IS FORGOTTEN WHEN WE ARE PLANNING A NEW INTERIOR SCHEME AND IT SHOULD BE CONSIDERED FIRST. PERHAPS THIS IS BECAUSE IT IS INTANGIBLE. WE CANNOT TOUCH IT OR FEEL IT IN THE WAY THAT WE CHOOSE A FABRIC, BY EXPLORING A RANGE OF SAMPLES. YET IT IS LIGHT THAT SETS THE MOOD AND GOVERNS WHAT WE SEE. WITH A LITTLE KNOWLEDGE OF THE NEW LIGHTING TOOLS AND DESIGN TECHNIQUES AT OUR DISPOSAL, AND AN UNDERSTANDING OF THE EXCITING EFFECTS THEY CAN CREATE, LIGHT BECOMES AN ESSENTIAL KEY TO UNLOCKING THE POTENTIAL OF OUR INTERIORS.

A WELL BALANCED
LIGHTING SCHEME IS
MADE UP OF THREE KEY
LIGHTING TYPES: A
FLATTERING GENERAL
LIGHT, TASK LIGHTING
THAT PERFORMS A
FUNCTIONAL PURPOSE
AND FEATURE LIGHTING
THAT CAN PUT DISPLAY
OBJECTS IN THE
SPOTLIGHT. IT IS THE USE
OF A VARIETY OF LIGHT
SOURCES AT DIFFERENT
INTENSITIES THAT GIVES
CHARACTER TO A ROOM.

tools of light

The true potential of lighting lies in the way in which it can transform an adequate space into something sensational. With more subtle and sophisticated lighting effects than ever before, we are now able to recreate the diversity of natural light and shade in our own living spaces. But while we spend time and creativity on our choice of fabric, pattern and colour, lighting is often forgotten. Yet it should be considered first. No matter how beautiful the decoration of your room, it will appear lack-lustre and two-dimensional without the dynamic of light. What is the point of a beautiful stone floor or a work of art if it is not lit to best effect? Equally, the most eye-catching light fitting will lose its appeal if it provides insufficient light by which to read or cook a meal.

A little forward planning is essential. It helps to think three-dimensionally and then focus your attention on a few fundamental points. Firstly, assess the space to be lit, how you wish to use it, its shape and size, and the mood you wish to create. Next, give thought to your decoration, your preferred colour scheme and choice of furnishings, whether contemporary, eclectic or traditional. Then, the detail. Consider your room's best features, whether architectural, such

as an elaborate cornice, or decorative, such as a striking painting or object. Less attractive aspects may be best unlit. Lastly, be aware of any practical restrictions such as limited access to a ceiling from the floor above. All these elements will influence the way you decorate with light.

Understanding the tools at your disposal is the key to a successfully lit interior. There are no fixed rules but it helps to divide lighting into its different elements, each of which can be used individually or in combination. Once you have a sense of which tool is best for which purpose, you can then be as creative as you wish in putting them together. Each lighting type gives its own character to a space and can be adjusted from day to night. Some rooms may need only one or two lighting types, while complex spaces may require more. The objective when lighting any room, however, is to build up your lighting scheme gradually so as to create a harmonious balance.

There are three basic types of light. General lighting (sometimes known as ambient light) provides overall brightness. It is extremely versatile and essential for everyday use. Placing it on a dimmer system provides flexibility.

Feature, or accent, lighting creates the highlights, directing attention to focal points such as a favourite piece of furniture, a centrepiece of beautiful roses, or an architectural element. Feature lighting can also transform display shelves and alcoves. Local rather than general, it acts as an additional layer in your lighting scheme, accentuating without upsetting the equilibrium.

Task lighting is designed for specific needs, such as food preparation in the kitchen, reading in bed, or applying make-up in the bathroom. It provides a strong localized light, its source usually hidden from view to avoid glare, leaving you free to adjust the general and feature lighting to suit your mood.

Traditionally, a lighting scheme often comprised a single fitting, such as a pendant light, which would be used in all three ways. Sometimes a table lamp would double up, providing general light as well as light to read by. But lighting designs now give us much more scope and by lighting several surfaces simultaneously, rather than all surfaces with a single source, interiors are brought instantly to life. We can now bring light exactly where we want it, dappling the floor or washing a wall.

There are six main lighting tools to consider: downlighters, uplighters, wallwashers, decorative lighting, colour and control. It helps to think of them in terms of the inspiring effects they can produce – from dramatic emphasis to gentle illumination - rather than as fixtures and fittings.

Downlighters are usually recessed into a ceiling, although they can be wall- or ceiling-mounted. As the name suggests, they direct light downwards, emphasizing whatever lies in their path, whether simply the floor or a table. The light is specific and direct and will create fairly strong shadows, particularly if a narrow beam is used to highlight a feature. With a wide beam, or when arranged as an array of twinkling ceiling lights, the effect is that of a more even, general light.

Uplighters wash the ceiling with light, which is then reflected back into the room as diffuse, even lighting. They create a wonderful sense of space and height when the ceiling is white or light in colour, but if the ceiling is dark, the amount of reflected light will be minimal. They also offer great flexibility and can be free-standing or wall-mounted, usually above eye level to avoid glare. In the form of a narrow

pinspot, recessed into the floor, an uplighter can also act as feature lighting, adding dramatic emphasis to an arch or column.

Wallwashers can be recessed or surface-mounted and are designed to cast light evenly across and down a wall. Whereas downlighters and uplighters place emphasis on the height and depth, wallwashers concentrate light on the vertical surfaces. By using the wall as a reflector, a wallwasher provides a gentle, diffuse general light if fitted with a frosted lens or a wide beam, but when used with a narrow beam it becomes a dynamic source of feature lighting. Positioning will also affect the overall impression. When set back, the effect is of diffuse light, but if placed close to the wall, decorative scallop shapes of light will play across the surface. And wallwashers are in their element when used to emphasize surface texture, such as rough brickwork.

Decorative lighting fulfils its main function in traditional interiors. Specific fixtures are sometimes required to reflect historical references, but these can be skilfully combined with modern designs as part of the overall scheme. For example, a period lantern in a hallway might be combined with a concealed

downlighter to either side. The lantern provides the visual focus, emitting light in all directions. When supplemented with downlighters, the lantern can be dimmed, providing a softer, more decorative effect while the downlighters do the work. Or table lamps might be paired with low-voltage spotlights, used to emphasize a decorative cornice. In this way, a lighting scheme can echo the style of an interior whilst taking advantage of the effects that modern lighting has to offer.

Nor should we forget the warm, flickering glow of firelight on a winter's evening, or the magical, shimmering style of candlelight, both of which are unrivalled as tools for creating atmosphere in our living spaces.

Artificial light comes in subtly contrasting shades, just as paint comes in myriad tones of white. The crisp white light of a low-voltage bulb is different to the glow of the standard tungsten bulb, used in everyday table lamps. The cool white light of a low-voltage halogen source is more compatible with daylight, but can be too harsh at night unless it is dimmed, when it takes on the warmth of candlelight. Conversely, during the day, lamplight always appears too yellow, but at night is warm and

inviting. Fluorescent light emits various shades of white ranging from a very cool, almost daylight tone, which can be quite harsh, to a warm, pink glow. Fluorescent light sources do not change colour as they are dimmed; they merely become less bright, which can sometimes make their light appear a little dull and almost grey.

The form of any light fitting is determined by the type of bulb it takes. Low-voltage bulbs in particular have revolutionized lighting design. Miniature compared with conventional mains-voltage fittings, they are most effective where the light source needs to be discreet, as in feature lighting. Task lights, such as the classic Tizio, use low-voltage fittings, too, for their fine optical precision. Fluorescents, on the other hand, by virtue of their linear design, produce a very even, flat light and can be used for uplighting or wallwashing, concealed if necessary behind a deep cornice or dedicated cover. As with all light fittings, a clear tungsten bulb with a bare filament will always produce sharp shadows whereas a frosted bulb or lens will produce a softer, more diffuse light. Clear bulbs are magical when used with a lantern or chandelier as the filament (wire in the centre of the bulb) creates a soft candlelight effect when

dimmed. But a table lamp fitted with a clear bulb will project the shadow of the shade on the ceiling, unlike a frosted bulb that gives out a soft overall light where shadows seem to merge.

The final tool in a skilful lighting scheme is control. With your lighting system separated onto different circuits, each element can be individually controlled and the whole composition balanced to achieve your desired effect. You may have pre-set controls in every room, programmed to suit different occasions. Or you may simply have a single dimmer switch for a change of mood from early to late evening. In either event, it is control that can both create atmosphere and change it in an instant, transforming a bright and airy workroom by day into a dramatic or intimate space to be enjoyed by night.

When used to best effect, light is never noticed, creating maximum impact with minimum intrusion. With the tools now at our disposal, the simplest of spaces can be infused with richness and depth, dimensions can be enhanced, structure highlighted and textures emphasized. Knowing how to use these tools in combination will provide you with a platform for your own creative ideas.

The narrow 10-degree focus from a recessed
spotlight above highlights grasses in a narrow
ceramic vase. The fall of the light creates a strong
pattern of light and shade, adding texture to a
simple arrangement.

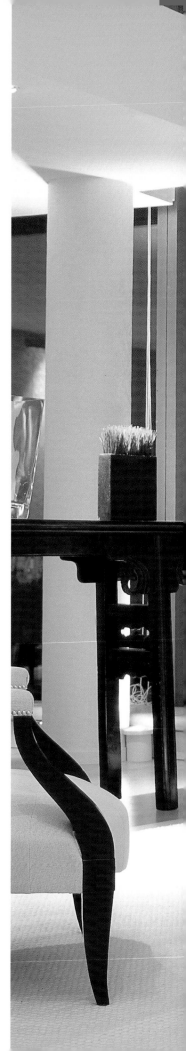

In a riverside apartment, a coffee table
becomes a focal point when highlighted with
rope lighting twisted around the base to
create a floating effect. Table lamps, just out
of view, provide general lighting in the form
of pools of light at floor level. In contrast, the
uplighters, positioned to either side of the
columns, throw light up these architectural
elements. When the exterior of the building
is lit, too, there is no need for curtains, or
even pictures, the view being the strongest
visual draw. With interior lights dimmed,
the outside comes inside.

*As the daylight fades, casting a blue
hue, supplementary kitchen lighting
is provided by localized under-
cabinet task lights, essential to
avoid working in one's own
shadow. At night they also help to
provide mood lighting.*

*Task lighting a counter can be as
appropriate for a vanity unit in a
bathroom as it is for a kitchen work
surface. Used above a basin (top
right), task lighting gives glamour
and sparkle to a marble surface and
chrome fittings but is useless for
facial lighting, as shadows are
accentuated. By introducing side
light (bottom right), either from
decorative fixtures or, in this case,
the reflected light of the lit niches,
unflattering downward light
is counteracted.*

Uplighters provide a soft, general light that is flattering to dinner guests. In the bay window of a dining room, recessed low-voltage uplighters frame the view as well as directing light upwards onto the ceiling, which acts as a reflector. A narrow-beam low-voltage downlighter makes a focal point of the roses and then filters through the glass tabletop, creating patterns on the floor beneath.

The frosted glass division between the glazing and the leather floor in a contemporary apartment is uplit from underneath. This form of lighting emphasizes architectural features, such as the slender columns which, decorated with silver leaf, provide an added lustre.

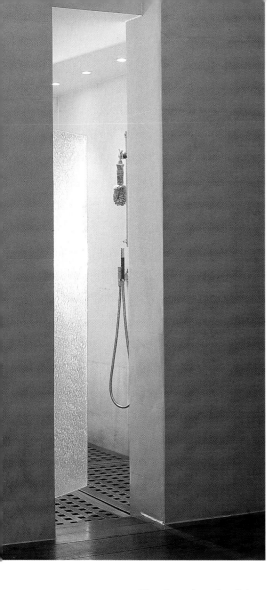

An expanse of cupboard doors
lends itself to wallwashing, which
can provide general light in a
kitchen by using the wall as a
reflector (below). It can be equally
effective in a bedroom with fitted
wardrobe doors. When arranged on
a separate switch, wallwashing can
also act as atmospheric feature
lighting. The simplest effect, shown
here, uses 40-degree beam angles
with frosted lenses to give softer arcs
(clear lenses will produce a sharper
pattern). The adjacent display unit
has a small, slimline, under-cabinet
light recessed into each niche.

Three low-voltage downlighters,
close off-set, skim down the back
wall of a shower, creating a
scalloped form of wallwash (above).
The outer bezel of the light fitting
should be 25-50 mm (1-2 in)
from the wall. The frosted shower
door appears to glow, backlit by
lights recessed into the side wall.
When used on its own, the
backlighting can double up as a
nightlight. When used undimmed,
it adds to the level of general light.
Downlighters are ideal for
bathrooms, where safety
considerations reduce the choice
of approved fixtures.

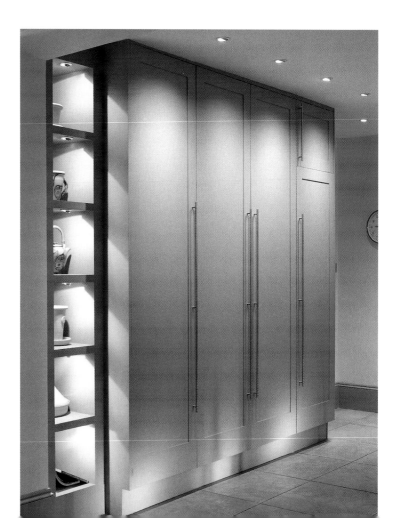

A combination of lights illuminates
these displays: downlighters are
used above the glazed units while
under-cabinet lights are set into the
timber shelves, each with a discreet
'eyelid', or glare guard, to shield
the source of light.

Side lighting not only fulfils a practical function on a stairway by providing safe passage; it also creates a strong pattern of light and shade. Low-level wash lights, positioned at every third step (above), are a more dramatic and effective approach to lighting a narrow stairway than a single overhead light. This scheme is particularly useful for lighting stairs to basements. Low-level wash lights can also be fitted to accentuate the route along a corridor (left) and are particularly effective on a polished wood floor. Used in combination with a high-level wash light on the opposite wall, they illustrate the added vitality that comes from layering light or any asymmetric play of light.

Pure downlight in a bathroom produces unflattering shadows on the face and should be counteracted by supplementary lighting. Low-voltage downlighters (left) focus on the shiny white marble surface of a vanity unit, which reflects light back and softens the effect. Under the vanity unit, which is cantilevered, a rope light is concealed to give a soft glow to the floor. This has a useful dual function as a night-light.

An option for mirror lighting is to use indirect light behind the mirror itself (above). This creates the effect of a 'frame of light', which, when reflecting off a white background, produces a flattering facial light.

An alternative to lamps in a living room is under-shelf lighting. Using a low-voltage miniature track, the light is concealed by a cantilevered timber shelf to create an eye-catching floating effect. Light is also bounced off the timber floor, adding additional light at low level. A medium-beam recessed low-voltage downlighter catches the orchids, casting shadows on the wall behind. The two effects work well together and demonstrate the importance of layering light.

Decorative fixtures play an important part in a lighting scheme, whether lanterns, standard lamps or table lamps. They can provide light at any height from overhead to low-level. Lanterns should always be used with a dimmer and never at full strength, as the light needs to be softened. The use of clear bulbs, rather than their frosted counterparts, will ensure sparkle. Shaded sources, such as table lamps and standard lamps, look better with frosted bulbs as they are used for soft, flattering, general light. In addition, if you use a clear bulb with a shaded lamp you will see the shadows of the shade carrier on the ceiling, so again a frosted bulb is preferable. Each interior requires a different look, so select the appropriate fixture in each case.

Directional lighting is an important part of any scheme and can be used in many different ways to create focus in a room. Side lighting, when surface-mounted, provides the best means of lighting the face. Uplighting dried twigs provides a diffuse, indirect light and a dramatic silhouette. Downlighting a Dale Chihuly glass sculpture with a recessed 10-degree spotlight makes it appear lit from within. The bookcase is simply wallwashed with recessed downlights angled towards the shelves. This is particularly successful for books but objects need to be positioned to the front of the shelf to avoid being in shadow, or, better still, lit from in front with a 'footlight' on the shelf, which will cast larger-than-life shadows on the wall behind. When more light is required in a room but adding yet another lamp would give the impression of a lamp shop, these techniques will provide interesting alternatives.

HIGHLIGHTING UNITES A
SPACE BY PROVIDING A
SENSE OF FOCUS. WITH
THE BACKGROUND
DIMMED, OUR EYES ARE
NATURALLY DRAWN TO
THE BRIGHTEST VISUAL
ELEMENT. THE CONTRAST
BETWEEN HIGHLIGHTS
AND LOWER LEVELS OF
LIGHTING IS AN
ESSENTIAL INGREDIENT
WHEN CREATING
ATMOSPHERE.

chapter 4

creating focus

Lighting excels in creating drama. A striking sculpture, a single flower or a decorative cornice, when given emphasis with light, provides a focus without which our living spaces feel bland and lifeless. Interiors are not static places; focal points created with light can guide us from one space to another, providing impetus and building momentum as well as bringing a favourite object into the limelight. With focus you can even make space more dynamic. By varying the effect and intensity of light in a long passageway, for example, and providing a dramatically spotlit feature at one end, proportions are immediately transformed. Every space can benefit from a focus to capture our attention and we need not be limited to interior spaces. A garden, when lit at night, creates an equally dramatic focus beyond our four walls, which is best appreciated with interior lights gently dimmed.

Knowing how to achieve a balance, by varying the different light levels and lowering the overall intensity, is instrumental in creating a sense of drama. This is demonstrated by natural light, which creates focal points, too. Think of the brightness of a shaft of light through a

skylight, or even a brightly lit window, both of which can make the darkest room appear light. It is the relative difference in contrast between light and shadow that provides the emphasis. In an interior, if an architectural feature, a prized possession or a focus of activity such as the dining table, is to be highlighted, then the surroundings are best illuminated by a lower general light. An artist uses the same technique when introducing both high- and lowlights in a painting. Getting the balance right is the key to any well-designed lighting scheme.

A photographer understands this process and will always take a light meter to measure the relevant intensities of light, thus ensuring the correct balance. Something that has a high reflective value, influenced by whether it is matt or gloss and the degree of colour saturation, may appear too intense and will burn out on film, whereas insufficient contrast will create a bland picture. The human eye is less sensitive than a camera (but far more skilful). While it is naturally attracted to the brightest point in a room, it provides infill light to soften any contrast. When lighting an interior we can apply the same principles.

Deciding when to use contrast is an important consideration. By night, feature lighting comes into its own. During the day, however, an even brightness is less tiring on the eye than continually looking from an intense source of light, perhaps from a desk lamp, to surroundings that may be in semi-darkness (this should be borne in mind when planning a work space).

The means by which to create focus is feature lighting which, for maximum effectiveness, should be clearly defined, precise and controlled separately from other light sources. If your focal point is an architectural detail, or a favourite painting, then the light source should be discreet, directing attention to the object being featured rather than providing a distraction. Only when the light source itself is the principal feature, such as a chandelier, should it be centre stage. By using dimmers to vary the balance of general and feature lighting, you can create theatrical effects, altering the atmosphere of a room as you wish.

In living and dining rooms, where we relax and entertain, feature lighting is an important ingredient. In this kind of environment,

decorative objects are for the most part a source of contemplation, making purpose-designed light sources invaluable. A beautiful urn will look magical, as if lit from within, when illuminated with a narrow-beam downlight. A painting can draw the eye when framed by combination up/downlighters to either side. Plants and flower arrangements are perfect subjects for focus, as light brings out the texture as well as the colour of leaves and flowers. An architectural element, such a decorative cornice, can be thrown into relief when highlighted by a recessed uplighter.

As well as showing off a room's best features, focus lighting can create a wonderfully intimate atmosphere for a dinner party. A single downlighter over the dining table will draw guests like moths to a flame. Enhanced with candlelight, it adds sparkle to glass and tableware, while a level of general light will provide infill, preventing shadows from falling on diners' faces. Pictures add interest in a dining room, too. For maximum flexibility, picture lighting should be arranged on a separate circuit from table and general lighting.

The idea of focus is rarely considered in secondary areas such as hallways and passages, staircases and bathrooms, which tend to be regarded as more utilitarian. Transitional spaces should be treated with equal importance, as they set the mood and link different spaces. There is no point lighting rooms dramatically and then linking them with a dull, uniformly lit hall. They should continue the mood.

Halls and stairways are often architecturally interesting, offering unusual perspectives, changes of level and features such as archways or curving walls. Both lend themselves to subtle lighting effects. Yet a central lantern is all too often the only light source, with little thought given to highlighting features that could make the space appear larger or features more interesting. The result is that the lighting is either too bright or too dim. Instead of a wall light, a small niche can provide focus as well as highlighting a beautiful object, or backlighting it to create a silhouette. Floorwashing staircase treads provides another decorative alternative, its strong low-level light giving emphasis to each step as well as improving safety. Sometimes

the shape of a stairway is sculptural in itself and can be accentuated with a combined up/downlighter. Often the most effective way to provide general light is by lighting each half-landing and then relying on the spill light to illuminate the rest. Adding focus as an extra layer provides the atmosphere.

Bathrooms can be transformed with feature lighting from a bright, functional space in the morning to a relaxing oasis in the evening. Using narrow-beam halogen fittings, you can create a focal point on a collection of pebbles or a picture, just as you would in a living space or dining area. When positioned over a bath or basin, the crisp white light will create added sparkle as it catches the water.

Feature lighting excels when used to focus on treasured possessions, whether displayed singly in glorious isolation or grouped on shelves, or in a specially designed cabinet. Feature lighting can take different forms depending on what is to be lit, from paintings to glass and ceramics. Taking two-dimensional objects, such as paintings, as a starting point, the traditional

A painting is highlighted with two fully adjustable low-voltage medium-beam spotlights of equal intensity (below). The darker side of the picture reflects less light and so appears less brightly lit. A narrow-beam low-voltage downlighter, recessed into the ceiling, makes a feature of the simple centrepiece on the dining table.

form of lighting is the picture light. Fittings with modern technology, low-voltage halogen light sources are very effective and can be concealed within traditional fittings using remote, flat transformers. The whiter light of halogen will produce a truer colour than traditional tungsten tubes. A successful effect, however, depends on a good throw of light, which in turn is determined by the length of the picture-light arm. This is often forgotten, and it is the reason why picture lights with a very slim and elegant appearance but a short arm are only suitable for lighting a small painting. Picture lights are best fixed immediately behind the frame, or frame-fixed. Wall-mounted lights are sometimes impractical; too often they are mounted at too high a level with the result that the wall, rather than the picture, is lit.

Spotlights, whether surface-mounted, track-mounted or fully recessed into the ceiling, are used to light a picture with a narrow pool of light, which can then be softened or diffused with lenses (they can also be added to reduce UV radiation for valuable pictures). Usually the

The enormous triptych installation by
John Virtue comprises one double-
height central element and two single-
storey pieces. These are lit from above
by a run of miniature recessed
high-level fibre optics at 300mm (1 ft)
centres, directed to focus on different
parts of the artwork. Fibre optics
facilitate maintenance over a double-
height space.

light source is low-voltage halogen, which
creates a clear, white light and provides good
colour rendering. Pictures with a noticeable
texture may look more dramatic if lit by a
spotlight that accentuates the paint surface. Any
reflections from a glazed frame are minimized
when a spotlight is used as an uplighter.

The most sophisticated form of feature lighting
is the framing projector, which can be used for
lighting paintings, prints and photographs,
producing spectacular results. When direct
lighting appears too harsh on a sculpture,
accentuating shadows that detract from its
appearance, a framing projector can provide an
alternative. Light is focused on the object alone,
casting no shadow on the wall from the frame
and allowing no overspill onto the background.
When lit in this way, pictures appear to be
magically lit from within and sculptures seem
to be suspended dramatically in midair. The
skill in this type of installation lies in the
dexterity of the specialist who cuts the copper
shield that masks the light to the correct shape.
This type of light fitting can even be used in
the garden, if the projector is concealed in a
waterproof housing.

The central double-height section of the mural receives supplementary lighting from the recessed floor uplights (far left and left). These need to be specifically designed for areas where they may be walked over. If used in close proximity to artworks, low-heat fixtures should be specified. Fibre optics can also be used as uplighters, providing the remote light source can be fitted in a convenient floor or wall space.

Three-dimensional objects, such as a flower display or glassware, have different lighting requirements. They can be backlit, silhouetted or thrown into relief, lit from one direction for surface texture or cross-lit for a truly three-dimensional effect. When lighting a bowl of flowers or a decorative object or sculpture, the same principles apply as for picture lighting. Spotlights can be used to highlight all three, but different sculptures may require the light to be directed at different angles. Glassware is especially receptive to light. If frosted and downlit, it will appear to hold the light as if lit from within. When lit with fibre optics from below, the object itself becomes the source of light (fibre optics, unlike low-voltage sources, have low heat emissions, so no damage will be done when an object is placed on top). A collection of Lalique glass, for example, would look spectacular lit in this way.

Another atmospheric technique is to cast an object into silhouette by backlighting it. Used with bronzes and sculptures with simple shapes, this can create a dramatic effect as it emphasizes the two-dimensional form of these three-dimensional works.

When properly lit, display alcoves or fitted shelves can provide a decorative focus that is sometimes just as effective as the objects displayed. Shelf lighting need not be relegated to a special collection in a living room. Even shelving in a bathroom or kitchen, with a more prosaic display of ceramic jars or beautiful shells, can become a special feature when given a subtle lighting effect.

With glass shelves, a single downlighter will radiate light through each shelf to dramatic effect. A collection of glassware, displayed in this way, will sparkle when lit with downlighters and will not cast shadows on the shelf below. Solid objects need to be carefully positioned to catch only some of the light, while allowing some to pass through to the shelf below.

If solid shelves are used, there are various options, from miniature, recessed low-voltage downlights to miniature track lights containing tiny festoon lamps. These can be arranged to create pools of highlight around objects when the bulbs are spaced, or an even light when the bulbs are positioned continuously. This kind of track can even be used at the back of a shelf to

silhouette a favourite possession. With glass, small low-voltage 'footlights', positioned in front, will both highlight a piece and throw a dramatic shadow onto the back wall.

With the right lighting, the simplest possession or breathtaking work of art can be turned into an eye-catching focal point. Within all well designed lighting schemes, feature lighting provides an extra layer, adding drama and contrast, a sense of surprise and discovery, and an intimate atmosphere. It emphasizes the best points in our interiors and plays down the worst. When it comes to introducing focus into our living spaces, feature lighting holds the key.

Objects in relief can be lit with a soft wallwash. A stone frieze of classical figures (left), set into a fireplace, is lit with low-voltage light sources with frosted lenses. These create a soft shadow and increase the three-dimensional nature of the frieze as well as provide an even, diffuse light. To light the fireplace, miniature fibre optic spotlights have been positioned to either side of the hearth. These are directed up to the underside of the mantelpiece, which in turn reflects light back onto the frieze.

A detail of the wall plaque illustrates how light falls, creating a three-dimensional display of light and shadow (right). A close-up view of the frieze (below) illustrates the effectiveness of combining toplight from soft wallwashers above with a delicate highlight from fibre optics at floor level.

A classical figure in a hallway is softly lit from above with a 24-degree low-voltage downlighter that accentuates the intricately carved drapery with patterns of light and shadow.

A marble urn, by comparison, is lit from above with a 10-degree beam. With the general light dimmed, the urn appears to be filled with light, an effect that puts into silhouette the carved relief on its outer surface.

Sculpture can be lit in different
ways to achieve different effects.
Crosslighting, while focusing on the
sculpture, allows the periphery spill
light to illuminate the surrounding
space (above right). Alternatively, a
framing projector can be used (left).
This type of low-voltage light
source is fitted with a metal mask,
carefully cut by a specialist, which
contours the outline of the sculpture
exactly. The spectacular effect is that
of an object floating in space. By
highlighting the object from an
oblique angle, the light source is
almost invisible from below. A table
lamp, located nearby, tempers the
surreal quality of light from the
projector alone.

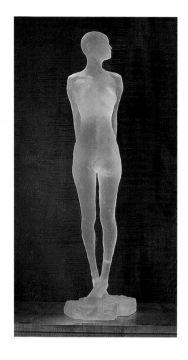

Glass can both absorb and refract light. When simply lit by two low-voltage downlighters, a glass sculpture will absorb the light and then refract it, giving the impression of being lit from within.

Concealed low-voltage track is an efficient means of lighting a display cabinet (left). Positioned on either side of the shelving, the track lighting highlights a collection of decanters. A black background ensures that the light is reserved entirely for the glass, causing the cut-glass facets to sparkle. Added drama comes from the Buddha in the foreground, which is uplit from below using a portable low-voltage uplighter, plugged into a nearby socket.

OVERLEAF

Niches can be lit in different ways according to the objects displayed. For ceramics, a miniature recessed low-voltage cabinet light is used with a small downstand (or metal shield) to conceal the light source. For glass displays, a miniature footlight, so-called because it sits at the front of the shelf, lights the glass, which then absorbs and refracts the light. An added effect is that of an enlarged, reflected image of the object, which is projected onto the back of the niche.

Flowers always respond well to light, and a narrow 10-degree spotlight, recessed in the skylight above, focuses light on the flowers. The gilding on the mirror has an added sheen as it reflects light from a nearby lantern.

The simple focus of a narrow 10-degree spotlight in the centre of a dining table is always dramatic (above). Unlike a wider beam, it ensures that the centrepiece is lit without casting any unflattering light on the surrounding diners. Windows at night act like mirrors, reflecting the room within. Adding exterior lighting solves this problem.

Light reflects off pale surfaces and is absorbed by dark areas, creating a different quality of illumination. A soft glow catches this painting which, being dark in colour, absorbs most of the light. The remainder is picked up by the red flowers, which provide a rich contrast with the moody background.

The staircase at its brightest is lit using low-glare, low-voltage miniature downlighters. To achieve the low-glare effect, the bulb is well recessed within the downlighter. A layering of light is introduced by highlighting the side of the stairs with small square floorwashers.

The mood can be changed dramatically by taking the emphasis away from the downlighters, which are now turned off. The main lighting comes from the floorwashers that light the stairs. As they shine through the balustrade, an interesting pattern of shadows is created on the facing wall.

Manipulating light now emphasizes a further feature. The eye is drawn to the end of the passage as a single downlighter highlights the vases of roses. This is more moody and atmospheric, as the play of shadows and light is unexpected.

BY DIMMING GENERAL
LIGHTING AND RAISING
FEATURE LIGHTS, A WIDE
VARIETY OF MOODS CAN
BE ORCHESTRATED
ACCORDING TO TASTE,
FROM LIGHT, BRIGHT AND
FUNCTIONAL AT ONE END
OF THE SPECTRUM TO
DEEPLY DRAMATIC AT THE
OTHER.

creating moods

We are all profoundly influenced by mood, that barely definable, abstract quality that makes us feel in tune with our surroundings. Lighting, more than any other element, allows us to manipulate the way our rooms look and feel. If you want guests to feel relaxed, light can achieve it. If you want a space that is exciting and stimulating, then light will make it happen. Light reflects the way we choose to live, even changing a mood from morning to evening. Most rooms now have dual functions, and lighting can enable spaces to perform this double act more effectively. A working kitchen, with practical task lighting for cooking, can become an intimate supper venue; or a child-friendly play area by day can be turned into a sophisticated living space by night. Light holds the key to a seamless transformation.

Mood and atmosphere are the 'special effects' of any lighting scheme, but the subtle levels required can only be determined at the fine-tuning stage. Once the various layers of lighting have been selected, we need to ensure a balance that will produce visual harmony, just as we layer textures and fabrics when decorating. Uplighting may need to be combined with downlighting, or table lights with spotlights, in just the right proportions.

Your requirements will vary from room to room. In a living room, table lamps may be necessary for general lighting and to ensure that people are seen in a soft flattering light. These can be combined with low-voltage feature lights to illuminate artwork and possibly a coffee table. In a kitchen, lamps are not practical for general lighting, which is far more effectively achieved by downlighters, wallwashing the front of the kitchen units, or uplighters, which provide a soft indirect light. These light sources can be combined with under-cabinet lighting for task light and perhaps a pinspot over a kitchen island for added focus.

Bathrooms and bedrooms require flexible lighting that is energizing in the morning and calming at night, with task lights for reading or around a mirror. In a bedroom, where there is less need for overall illumination, the bed itself can become the focus, appearing to float on a pool of light when rope lights are subtly concealed under the bed platform. Downlighters can be focused on a decorative object or a curtain treatment for extra atmosphere. With each effect controlled separately, you can orchestrate the mood you wish to create with a setting for every occasion.

The principal way in which we control lighting is by dimming the various levels in relation to each other. General lighting, whether in the form of table lamps, uplights or downlights, should be controlled separately from feature lighting. By day, relative contrasts are less marked. When general lighting is at its maximum strength, it will achieve a fairly even light throughout a room. By night, the way to create atmosphere and mood is to dim general lighting to a low level and raise feature lighting. For maximum effect, as intense as a Caravaggio painting, the contrast between different light sources will be high; for a soft, inviting light, similar to that produced by candlelight; the contrast between feature and general lighting will be less marked.

Mood and atmosphere are very subjective and have an effect on how we feel. If we have had a hectic day in a brightly lit office, coming home to a softly lit environment can have a very calming effect, helping us to relax and reducing stress. If the lighting is more dramatic, creating positive areas of brightness and darkness, an energetic and dynamic atmosphere is created. This is perhaps more appropriate for a party, as the low levels of overall light prevent activities such as reading or keyboard work. While light

Pools of light supplement the natural daylight that pours in through the window of a manor house hall, creating a bright, airy atmosphere. A narrow-beam light source highlights the sculpture on the central hall table, while miniature spotlights, concealed between the beams of the balcony, throw light onto walls and floors. To the right, next to the chair, a low-voltage portable uplighter illuminates the rafters and accentuates the rough plaster.

is the key to changing mood, the right levels of contrast are the means to success, achieved by controlling each lighting effect individually.

The wonder of light is its ability to transform a space, literally at the touch of a button. This is something that interior decoration can never do on its own. By focusing on what is to be seen, light can screen out what is not, by leaving these areas in darkness. But to control individual effects with a dimmer can result in numerous buttons and large unsightly control plates. Each button needs to be operated separately to achieve the desired mood, and this can sometimes be tedious when you want to re-create a favourite combination. We can draw on lessons learned in hotels and restaurants, where it is essential to realize an exact mood each night. The solution is to pre-set the lighting. This effectively means using dimmers that are located remotely. Each type of lighting effect is adjusted once and memorized for each setting. The switch plate has just four buttons to represent four different moods or scenes. In addition, an on/off button is provided and in some instances a 'raise and lower' button, which allows the scene to be fine-tuned further. Each scene button represents a memorized level for each of the effects you wish to create.

Scene one is usually bright, to be used on a dull day to compensate for overcast skies. Most of the lights will be adjusted to full brightness and some of the very discreet effects of feature lighting, which only work when light levels are low, may be programmed to 'off'. We move into early evening with scene two, set with a slightly lower level of light. Low-voltage halogen beams, with their crisp white light, may be dimmed to soften their appearance while task lighting is left slightly higher so that cooking can still take place in the kitchen, for example. For entertaining, scene three is suitably atmospheric. Dimming the general light to a lower level and raising the level of feature lighting increases the contrast. This can also be effective when a kitchen is to be transformed into a dining area, allowing pots and pans to disappear into the background. For special occasions or after dinner, scene four can be more moody still, introducing a sense of theatre. It can also double up as an economy setting, by providing night lights in a hallway, or when viewing television in a living room.

From morning to night, from relaxed to dramatic, from informal to theatrical, we can now change our interiors in an instant, with lighting tailor-made to our favourite moods.

The spiral staircase, which connects a contemporary living area to the mezzanine above, becomes a sculpture within the space when lit by three uplighters recessed into the floor below (right). Located at high level, a low-voltage spotlight focuses on the picture and creates sufficient reflected light to illuminate the treads. Both the bookcase and glass sculpture are lit with a recessed low-voltage downlight.

In addition to the feature lighting of the glass
statue (above), table lamps provide soft general
lighting, the most flattering choice next to the
sofas. By controlling the elements of feature
lighting and general lighting separately, different
moods can be created – one for early evening
drinks, an other for after-dinner coffee.

The various layers of lighting in a mezzanine living space include soft lamplight and picture lighting. Downlighters, centred on each pair of handles on the kitchen cabinets, provide both general light and an unusual form of focus. The glass screen, flowers and sculpture have downlights located directly above. Controlled separately, they form almost a visual barrier to the kitchen units behind. A low-voltage miniature track, concealed under the bar counter, adds a further dimension and highlights the leather floor. By orchestrating each of these effects individually, a variety of moods can be achieved, in this case on a pre-set dimmer system, from a light and functional mood to late-night drama.

The change of mood that can be created by light is illustrated by a group of orchids seen in daylight and then in evening light (above). Illuminated by natural light flooding through large windows, the orchids cast soft shadows on the wall behind, but when lit from below at night, their shadows are more sharply defined and dramatic.

A soft wallwash, using low-voltage directional fittings with frosted lenses, and the fibre optics used to highlight the fireplace, contrast with the asymmetric general light of the conventional standard lamp and internally lit side tables. Each effect in this living room is controlled separately, again on a pre-set lighting system, in order to change the mood from early to late evening.

A narrow-beam light source focuses attention on the centrepiece of a dining table and creates sparkle on glasses and silverware alike. When the general background lighting is subdued, the dining table immediately feels more intimate.

Even a simple display on a table (below) can be functional by day and dramatic by night when lit with narrow-focus light sources that can be controlled separately.

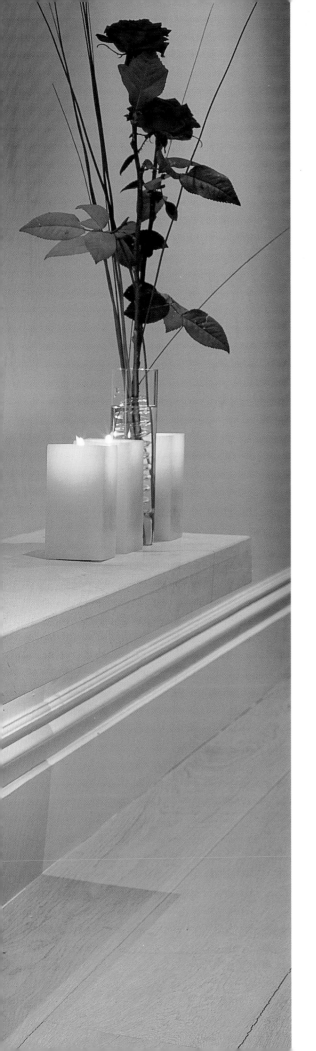

Candlelight and firelight provide far more than light and heat. More than anything else, they create atmosphere, with their dancing flames and long, flickering shadows. The rich, golden cast of firelight is welcoming and reassuring while candlelight brings a sense of intimacy. A miniature low-voltage track is concealed beneath the stone hearth to create a floating effect.

The bedhead forms part of a screen that encloses the shower (right). The recessed alcove, which acts as a display shelf, is lit with miniature track that provides a soft, general light and also acts as a bedside light. Lit by a ropelight concealed around the base, the bed seems to float, especially when other light sources are dimmed, so creating a magical highlight (below).

The dynamic view of a lit terrace replaces what would otherwise have been a black void and removes the need for curtains (above). A low-voltage miniature track has been used inside, under both the step and the shelves, to give a sense of lightness. Uplighters, concealed above the shelves, can be raised to produce a bright, general light or dimmed for a subdued, soft light to the pitched ceiling. The shelves are lit by sculptural objects, light forms in their own right.

General light, created from beam-mounted uplighters, catches each of the timber dowels in a country bedroom (right) so that they appear almost as light sources themselves. On the crossbeams, small low-voltage floods emphasize the pitched ceiling (above), in contrast to the more traditional effects from table lamps at low level.

A brick vaulted cellar has narrow-voltage downlighters discreetly integrated into the vaulting. They have a functional value by highlighting the bottles as well as the central table, essential when selecting the wine and checking the colour. These downlights can be dimmed to a candlelight glow when the space becomes a party venue.

PATTERNS ARE CREATED
WHEN LIGHT SHINES ON,
OR THROUGH, AN
OBJECT IN ITS PATH.
RANGING FROM SOFT
SCALLOP SHAPES TO
GRAPHIC STRIPES,
PATTERNS CAN BE
DELIBERATELY DESIGNED
OR PURELY INCIDENTAL.

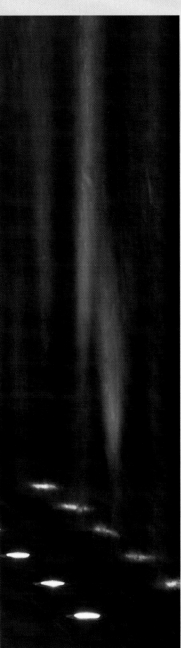

patterns with light

We have only to think of patterns in nature – the spiralling forms of seashells, the undulating edge of waves on the shore, the striations in the grain of wood – to recognize that pattern is all around us. Just as pattern affects our lives, it influences our interiors, transforming our appreciation of colour and texture, adding rhythm and movement or suggesting order and calm. In the form of soft, fluid outlines, pattern has the power to relax, while a bold graphic statement is energizing. It is a fundamental ingredient of decoration, breaking up strong shapes and plain surfaces and giving character and depth to a room.

Pattern is not only introduced through fabric and wallpaper. Light, too, creates an array of patterns through an interplay of light and shadow, from fragmented, kinetic and frosted patterns to rounded arcs, directional lines and projected abstract shapes.

Patterns of light fall into two main categories. The first occurs when an object lies in the path of light, casting a shadow beyond. This form of pattern-making is unpredictable and serendipitous, its permutations many and varied. We can take our inspiration from the natural world where, when sunlight strikes rippling water, flickering patterns are reflected up into trees along the water's edge. In the same way, if an artificial light source is directed onto water – a pool, fountain or waterspout – attractive reflections will pattern surrounding walls; a narrow spotlight, placed above a bath, will also create dancing patterns on the ceiling. Just as light shines through the leaves of a tree to create dappled patterns of light and shade below, so a low-voltage uplight, positioned behind foliage, will create patterns on the wall and ceiling. This looks effective both on an indoor surface and on the walls of a terrace outside. The pattern will depend on the type of foliage, whether soft and open like an olive tree or ficus, or angular and dramatic like a palm. The difference of effect lies in the ratio of light to shadow.

Any perforated material, when lit from behind or within, will decorate nearby surfaces with pattern, from linear stripes and arabesques to starbursts and pinpoints. The slats of a blind, for example, will create ordered bands across a polished floor. A pierced metal lantern will shower shooting stars on walls and ceilings, while light shining through a carved Moorish screen will inscribe its abstract outlines on walls and floors. An industrial metal staircase with perforated treads – the type often reclaimed for contemporary living spaces – can throw tiny pinpricks of light on surrounding surfaces when lit from above. An exciting alternative with a wooden staircase would be to floorwash the treads, which will cast shadows from the banisters onto the opposite wall. Contemporary wire-mesh sculpture can create fantastic effects whereby the pattern becomes more important than the object. When lit, the sculpture vanishes, leaving an echo of its shape on the wall behind. Depending on the angle of light, the pattern can be distorted from total realism, when lit front-on, to Baconesque abstraction when lit at an acute angle.

Glass, too, is a great pattern-maker. A frosted-glass table can be lit from above with a low-voltage downlighter to create a delicate tracery of reflected light on the ceiling while refracted light draws abstract designs on the floor below. Similar patterns are achieved by lighting glassware on display shelves from the front, and an engraved glass shade will cast shadows that echo its design. Light is refracted through the glass to create a pattern on the wall behind (the depth and complexity of pattern will vary depending on the engraving or frosting). With all these effects, when fixtures are fitted with a

Pattern making with light can take many forms. Downlighting with a powerful light source above a metal staircase creates abstract patterns on the side wall (left) as light filters through the perforated treads. Dots of light with a soft halo effectively decorate the polished plaster wall with light (right).

clear bulb, patterns will be crisply defined; the use of a frosted bulb will create softer shadows.

The second type of pattern making occurs when light hits an opaque surface, which then reflects light back. This is a more defined form of pattern-making that can be controlled and manipulated to striking effect. The play of light can affect our interpretation of a surface. With a soft wallwash, the fittings offset and directed towards the wall itself, a plain white wall will appear two-dimensional, lit by an even light. By contrast, the whole nature of the wall can change if the light fittings are placed very close to it and also directed downwards. Instead of providing a soft wash, the light makes more of a statement, grazing close to the surface and creating a strong visual pattern of pronounced arcs across the top. The narrower the beam, the more emphatic the pattern.

A more dramatic variation can be achieved in reverse, by using close-offset uplighting. With the arcs at floor level, the eye is drawn upwards by vertical shafts of light that graze the surface to a pool of soft, reflected light on the ceiling. These effects have a practical application as well as a decorative one. By emphasizing the vertical plane of the wall, this form of lighting can

minimize the effects of a low ceiling. It will also exaggerate any undulations on the surface. If your wall is of brick or stone, its texture will be enhanced, but if you have uneven plaster, this is best wallwashed from a distance, which will provide a flatter light.

Linear pattern-making can emphasize the horizontal, as well as the vertical dimensions of a room. Another wall-light technique can create an intriguing halo effect, with concentrated light at high level that gradually fades out towards the base. This is achieved by using a continuous source, such as miniature tungsten track for a soft light, or overlapping fluorescents for a cooler light. It is an effect that works very well in contemporary spaces, where light can be concealed between wall and ceiling and so appears to replace the traditional cornice.

The best method of illumination to use when creating patterns will depend on the interior. A smoothly plastered wall may take on a life of its own with a scalloped arc pattern from close-offset downlighters, but if the interest lies in the texture and material or colour of the wall, then a more even wallwash will emphasize its best features. A tiled wall at the back of a shower or bath is a good background for a scalloped

effect, as is a venetian slatted blind in a kitchen, bringing vitality to more practical living spaces that can often be overlooked. A wood-panelled hall or study, however, would be better lit with an even wash of light so as not to detract from the grain of the wood.

Changing from moment to moment and from sunrise to sunset, the effects of light and shade are something we almost take for granted. Yet patterns of light can literally change our perception of the surfaces that surround us. By animating walls, floors and ceilings with myriad designs, pattern-making is yet another facet of lighting that can enrich our living spaces.

*The underside of a metal stairway (page 112)
is highlighted almost as a sculptural element
within the space. Narrow streaks of light are
created by low-heat uplighters, which are located
close to the polished plaster wall, while the
strong downlighting provides the functional
light source.*

*Lighting a frosted glass staircase from below
(page 113) creates strong lateral stripes,
visually increasing the width of the space.
The frosted glass, when illuminated, makes
an emphatic contrast with the metal
surrounds of each tread and creates an
exciting transition between different levels.*

Glass and light together have great potential for producing pattern. A striking glass floor, uplit from below with a low-voltage light source (below and right), delineates the boundaries of a contemporary interior with a border of frosted stripes. Strongly directional, this pathway of light in turn projects a radial pattern on the surrounding metal upstand. The plate-glass window acts as a mirror to the patterns of light within as well as looking out onto a lit urban landscape.

Fragmented patterns can decorate surrounding walls more imaginatively than any wallpaper. The light effects produced by a Moroccan lantern are at their best when a clear bulb is used, as the projected patterns are crisp and not diffused. The dish of spices in the foreground is lit with a single low-voltage light source to emphasize the warm colours and create an alternative focus to the abstract patterns that are scattered over the wall.

A glass wall sconce, engraved with a trailing grapevine, projects a soft reflected pattern of grape clusters onto the back wall, where they appear as enlarged shadows. The frosted effect of the engraving creates less defined shapes.

The contrast between lit and unlit steps creates a graphic, striped pattern of light and shadow down a stone spiral staircase that leads to the cellar below.

Light from a wide-beam low-voltage spotlight, falling onto a collection of wine boxes, creates unusually dramatic blocks of light and shadow (right).

Pattern can be interpreted in many ways. Ginger jars, thrown into silhouette, form an effective frieze on a high kitchen shelf when lit by a linear light source such as a low-voltage track. Located behind the objects and along the base of the shelf, it lights the wall more strongly than the objects, which emphasizes the curved outlines of the jars to dramatic effect.

Atmosphere is achieved in a country kitchen by clever lighting. Downlighters, concealed as task lighting over the counters, throw light onto the copper pots (above and left).

Perspex shelves present a strong horizontal pattern when individually edge-lit with low-voltage track lighting.

The graphic lines of the edge-lit shelves form the backdrop to a home office. The light from the shelves is reflected in the polished surface of the hardwood desk, and localized task lighting is achieved using two downlighters.

DECORATING WITH
LIGHT IS AN UNDER-
ESTIMATED EFFECT, YET
THE POWERFUL
COMBINATION OF LIGHT
AND COLOUR IS A WAY OF
PRODUCING STUNNING
EFFECTS BY SIMPLE
MEANS. A WASH OF
COLOURED LIGHT ON
THE BLANK CANVAS OF A
WHITE WALL CAN CREATE
A TOTALLY DIFFERENT
MOOD – WITHOUT
HAVING TO REDECORATE.

coloured light

We all perceive colour in our own way. In part this is due to our physiological make-up, but it is also shaped by our own personal experiences. Inspiration for colour is all around us – in the landscape, in flowers, even in food. Wherever light is strong there are dazzling combinations of colour: the blue of the Mediterranean, the bright colours of Africa, the vibrant hues of India and Latin America. Colour adds flavour to life and richness to our surroundings. By using the three primary colours and controlling them individually, any shade can be created.

Light and colour are inextricably linked, for light is the means by which we perceive the rainbow colours of the spectrum. Without light there would be no colour. There are three pure colours in light – red, blue and green. When mixed together in pairs, these make the three secondary colours of yellow, cyan and magenta. Combining either the three primary or three secondary colours produces pure white light. Objects do not possess inherent colours of their own. When we see a red rose, it does not mean that in reality the rose is red. It simply means we perceive it as that colour. What we think we see is in fact the colour that the object reflects away from itself. When a ray of sunlight strikes a rose, the flower absorbs all the rays of the

spectrum except red. It is the red ray that the rose reflects back and which we pick up. The type of light in which it is seen affects the appearance of colour. A cooler, whiter light, such as fluorescent, will tend to bring out the blues and greens as it has a greater intensity of these colours in the spectrum. The more autumnal earth colours will seem lacklustre under a cool light as the spectrum has less yellow. By comparison, these tones are enhanced by a tungsten source, which has more yellow in the spectrum and therefore brings out the richer browns, reds and yellows but makes the blues and greens appear dull. A tungsten halogen source, which produces a whiter light than standard tungsten bulbs, often provides the best mid solution as it enhances most of the colour spectrum more evenly. It provides a truer quality of light and better colour rendering, which is why it is often used in interiors and to light artwork.

Not only is the light source important when it comes to reflecting colour values accurately, light is also the means by which we can introduce colour directly into our living spaces. Instead of painting a room with flat colour, imagine decorating your walls with luminous light. The work of American artist Dan Flavin

illustrates the potential of coloured light and its ability to dissolve boundaries. His vocabulary is a range of simple, unadorned, commercially produced, fluorescent light fixtures and tubes in rainbow colours, as well as cool and warm shades of white. Designers, too, are integrating coloured light into our public spaces. St Martin's Lane, the hotel in London designed by Philippe Starck, is the first hotel in which guests can select their own lighting tone: a different colour for a different mood. You make your choice and a wall-mounted switching station bathes you in coloured light. At night the hotel façade presents an ever-changing lightbox, all part of a desire to create a sensory experience with colour. Even television screens are fitted with mood settings that provide ambient light in different hues.

Coloured light is used to therapeutic effect in health and beauty spas, as different colours are thought to create different moods and so enhance the effectiveness of the treatment. The hot colours of the spectrum are invigorating, tonics that vitalize and shake us awake. Cool shades absorb, soothe and tranquillize.

With coloured light we can change not only the mood but also the apparent shape and size

Aquariums are now often installed as an alternative to a picture. An aquarium, built into the wall (right), is reflected in the dining table in the foreground and adds a bluish hue to the room, which contrasts with the red roses.

of our rooms as colours recede and advance. The way in which our perception of colour is affected by light, and the way in which colour affects our perception of space, is critical when it comes to interior design. Blue can increase a sense of spaciousness – think of the sky and sea – but in a room that receives little natural light, blue can seem cold and clinical. Red is warm and welcoming when used in small doses but a large expanse can be overwhelming.

By changing the light source, or by introducing a colour filter, you can create endless permutations on the blank canvas of a white wall (although it is worth remembering that when using a coloured light, anything in its path, or in the path of its reflections, will take on the same hue). Fibre optics fitted with colour wheels, or recessed colour-changing LEDs (light-emitting diodes), can literally change the colour of your walls at the touch of a button. For fun, these light sources can be run as a sequence to create a kaleidoscope of continually changing colours. With the light source concealed, all you are aware of is the magical effect of colour. As an alternative, for static colour impact a fluorescent with a colour 'sleeve', or a coloured glass filter over a downlighter, is effective. Dichroic glass filters

present yet another possibility. Fitted with multi-mirrored reflectors that direct light forward and draw heat back, they create a concentrated, slightly cooler beam of light which can be angled so that the projected colour is reflected on the glass.

In a contemporary space, which might take a stronger, more dramatic lighting scheme, a coloured light on a wall of the same colour can provide even greater intensity. For example, using a blue light of similar tone on a blue wall will increase visual saturation. The closer the colour of the light to the wall colour, the more dramatic the result, whether it is a continuous, soft wash from a colour-sleeved fluorescent or the more intense beam from a glass-filtered downlighter. Fluorescent tubes installed as part of a wall-mounted light box of coloured gels or filters can become an artwork in their own right, one in which the design can be varied by changing the filters.

The effect of light through coloured glass – a stained glass window or coloured lantern – can create stunning but more random effects, showering coloured lights across both walls and floors. Backlit with colour, a frosted glass screen used as a room divider, or as a side panel in a

bathroom, or as a splashback in a kitchen, will take on a totally different appearance. Coloured fluorescent tubes concealed above and below will provide a theatrical glow. This effect looks best when the light is backed by a white wall to increase reflection. Low-voltage track, when concealed behind the top of the glass and fitted with colour filters, will provide a wonderful scalloped wash of atmospheric coloured light. If access is a problem, fibre optics are a good choice and also allow for a change of colour.

For a truly dynamic colour-changing effect, edge-lighting glass with fibre optics or LEDs provides a spectacular solution. Edge lighting effectively places the light at one end of the glass. It then travels through the inside of the glass to the other end. To ensure evenness of effect, a strip of clear glass should precede the light source, as the colour will be strongest at the edges. When using LEDs, the primary colours of red, blue and green need to be located close together and then controlled individually, so as to allow any colour in the spectrum to be created. Fibre optics, on the other hand, use a colour wheel at the light source and the number of colours on the wheel limits the result. Both systems are equally effective and would work successfully with glass

panels. The only difference lies in the choice of changing colour and the ease of maintenance. Fibre optics can also be used as recessed uplighters to illuminate a wall, the light changing colour to give a variety of effects. Imagine the drama in a long corridor.

Lighting techniques are often appropriated from the theatre in order to bring additional colour and drama into our living spaces. One example is that of projecting an image onto a surface. Using a low-voltage projector fitted with a mask or 'gobo' cut to a specified outline, coloured patterns can be cast onto walls or ceilings. Designs can be as imaginative as you wish but the irregular shapes of leaves, water ripples or clouds are most effective. Used beneath a skylight, or on a courtyard wall that can be viewed from inside as well as outside, the effect can be sensational.

Introducing colour with light can transform our living spaces. It provides a magical paintbox of possibilities, from the subtlest wash of gentle hues, which dissolves boundaries, expands space and creates a relaxing, therapeutic atmosphere, to the most theatrical special effects. Have fun with colour.

Fibre-optic uplighters, recessed into the floor, are used to paint the curves of an arched ceiling with coloured light. The addition of a colour wheel allows up to four different colours to be selected. This lighting scheme is especially effective with a change of direction halfway down the corridor, achieved by installing the uplighters on opposite sides but overlapping in the centre.

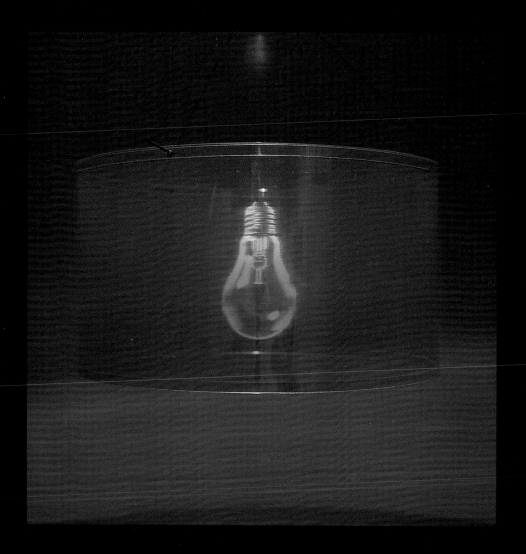

At one end of a dressing room (left), a visual joke is played. The actual light source is a narrow-beam low-voltage downlighter which, when switched on, illuminates the shade of a pendant light. A hologram of a light bulb magically appears. At a distance the hologram appears green in colour but as one gets closer it takes on a red hue, making colour the central focus (above). At low level, small square floorwashers emphasize the wood floor of the dressing room, creating an extra layer of light.

A frosted glass splashback to a kitchen counter (right) can take on a different hue by fitting a coloured 'sleeve' externally over a fluorescent tube. Here, the magenta-coloured light contrasts with the wooden Japanese bowls. If there is enough space to fit more than one tube, a choice of colours can be made available.

The colour of curtains and sheers in a bedroom (far left) is reinforced by a wash of coloured light from recessed fluorescents below them, fitted with 'sleeves' of lilac-coloured gel. The lilac hue is picked up by the reflective surface of the silver-leaf wallpaper and accentuates the depth of colour on the deep purple bottles (left).

Apart from the virtuoso effects of using coloured light, colour and light can work together in other simpler ways. Small touches of colour, such as a deep pink leather frame, can add highlight to any room, especially when emphasized by recessed downlighters. Coordinating pink lampshades glow when lit from within, reinforcing the theme.

Lighting can emphasize depth of colour. Two low-level uplighters skim a red textured wallcovering while the narrow focus of a recessed directional downlighter highlights a sculpture of Buddha. The contrast between the dark patina of the bronze and the rich red of the background is accentuated as red tones reflect more light than dark tones.

3

creating outdoor drama

LIGHTING RECLAIMS OUR GARDENS, EXTENDING OUR ENJOYMENT OF THEM BEYOND DAYLIGHT HOURS AND THROUGHOUT THE SEASONS. SO WHEN DESIGNING A GARDEN, WHETHER LARGE OR SMALL, WHETHER TRADITIONAL OR CONTEMPORARY, IT IS WORTH CONSIDERING AT THE OUTSET HOW LIGHT CAN EXTEND ITS SCOPE. JUST AS WITH OUR INTERIORS, LIGHTING CAN ALTER PERSPECTIVE, ENHANCE TEXTURE, INTRODUCE COLOUR AND CREATE ATMOSPHERE. WHILE FULFILLING A PRACTICAL FUNCTION BY DELINEATING PATHWAYS AND ILLUMINATING STEPS, IT CAN ALSO CREATE DRAMA BY HIGHLIGHTING A STATUE OR THROWING PLANTING INTO SILHOUETTE. IT REINFORCES THE MAGICAL PROPERTIES OF WATER, ACCENTUATING THE SPARKLE OF A SIMPLE WATERSPOUT OR A CASCADING FOUNTAIN. IT CAN EVEN SIMULATE MOONLIGHT SHINING THROUGH TREE TOPS. FILTERED THROUGH A PERGOLA OR CANOPY OF CLIMBING ROSES, LIGHTING ENHANCES OUTDOOR ENTERTAINING, TURNING A SIMPLE ALFRESCO MEAL INTO A SPECIAL OCCASION.

SUCCESSFUL LIGHTING IN THE GARDEN DEPENDS UPON ACHIEVING A HARMONIOUS BALANCE BETWEEN WHAT IS LIT AND WHAT IS LEFT IN SHADOW. BY ORCHESTRATING THE LIGHTING OF ENTRANCES AND EXITS, THE PLANTING, ARCHITECTURAL FEATURES AND, ABOVE ALL, WATER, WE CAN CREATE A WHOLE SPECTRUM OF MOODS OUTSIDE THE HOME AS WELL AS INSIDE, FROM PEACEFUL CONTEMPLATION TO THEATRICAL DRAMA.

IDEAS FOR LIGHTING STEPS AND PATHWAYS – 174

CREATING YOUR OWN LIGHT SHOW – 182

SPECIAL EFFECTS: FLOODING WALLS WITH COLOUR – 180

CANDLELIGHT AND WATER: A MAGICAL FUSION – 185

ADDING DRAMA WITH LIT WATER FEATURES – 186

WITH THE MEDIUM OF
LIGHT, A GARDEN CAN
BECOME AN OUTDOOR
ROOM TO BE ENJOYED
ALL YEAR ROUND. BY
HIGHLIGHTING A FEW
KEY FEATURES, FROM
A TREE OF RIPENING
FRUIT TO DECORATIVE
PLANT CONTAINERS,
LIGHT CAN SUPPLY A
SENSE OF MAGIC TO
THE SMALLEST
GARDEN OR ROOF
TERRACE.

chapter 8

small gardens and roof terraces

A garden is a source of pleasure during the day, yet it is often forgotten at night. On scented summer evenings, even the smallest garden can be transformed into a magical outdoor room, while on winter nights, if the garden is lit, it will provide interest and excitement inside, drawing the eye and enhancing a feeling of space. With a well-designed scheme, a small garden or roof terrace can be enjoyed whatever the time of day and whatever the season.

Just as contemporary interior design has seen huge changes, a similar revolution has happened in garden design, opening up greater potential for lighting ideas. In the modern, urban garden there is often less planting and more emphasis on architectural landscaping. Water features have greater prominence, now that water can be circulated by computer-controlled systems, and its light-reflecting qualities are welcomed along with its ability to muffle the sounds of a busy street. Lighting can be as simple as soft washes of light on the exterior of a building, combined with illuminated steps and uplit foliage, the light sources concealed by shrubs. But equally it can now be much more adventurous, especially when integrated at the earliest stages of garden design, allowing you to alter the light levels according to mood, or to highlight different

aspects from summer to winter. In fact, light is an essential tool in creating the contemporary 24-hour garden.

Outdoor spaces can reflect our individual styles and preferences in the same way as our interiors, and the way they are lit can echo and reinforce a particular theme. A wildflower garden will be softer and less predictable than a more formal, minimal design and so requires a more random approach, with flexible lighting that can be moved as plants come into flower and the seasons change. A contemporary roof garden in Japanese style will benefit from precision light effects. It will be more rigorous in its design and may incorporate a water feature, so lighting should be treated in a more formal manner to enhance these elements. In town gardens, herbaceous borders have often given way to a more structured use of space, perhaps using decking and architectural plants to make a statement, so recessed uplighters will be more effective than soft wall lights.

In the same way that you might approach a lighting design for an indoor room, it is worth giving a little thought to how you will use your outdoor room and how different areas will relate to different functions: a terrace for

al fresco meals; the practical consideration of well-lit doors, steps and pathways; the visual focus of a special feature or a view framed with light. The aims and objectives when planning garden lighting are the same as for an interior, but the way you achieve them will vary, not least because there is no longer a ceiling. The same tools of light are at our disposal in terms of general, task and focus lighting, which can be layered to create exciting yet harmonious effects. Uplighting, spotlighting and silhouetting all have their place in the garden. Walls can be grazed with light for added texture, and plants can create pattern with their shadows. In the garden, however, there is less need for high levels of general lighting and more scope for decorative focus. Above all, the football stadium approach, with its glaring floodlights, is to be avoided. A garden is much more magical when small pools of light appear within the darkness, its mystery created by unlit and lit areas.

A terrace with garden seats and a table is the centre of attraction in many gardens in the evening and as such is the first priority. The desired effect is that of a room outdoors, and this can be achieved by layering gentle background lighting with focus lighting over the table and by bringing up the lighting levels around the perimeters of the garden. Lit in this way, a terrace becomes a perfect spot for entertaining. If immediately outside the house, a terrace will be lit to a degree by the overspill of light from inside. Decorative wall lights to either side of French windows will provide subtle general light; alternatively, recessed or miniature low-voltage spiked uplighters are especially effective when reflected off pale adjacent walls and provide a soft, flattering light around the seating area. Again, if the terrace is next to the house or there is a tall tree close by, place a spotlight with a narrow, 4-degree beam at a high point about 6 metres (18 feet) away so that it focuses on the table, in the same way that you would arrange focus lighting in a dining room. This will create a pool of light in the centre. If you do not have an appropriate fixing point, candles or storm lamps can create a similar effect. Lighting on the terrace itself needs to be balanced with lighting a few metres away, perhaps using a lit trellis or lighting through plants to avoid a feeling of exposure. Think, also, of lighting one feature in the distance as a visual focus to provide interest.

Roof terraces can draw on lighting ideas for terraces on ground level but have an additional advantage in that they can be lit from below as well as from above. Uplighting through glass blocks, set into a wooden deck, creates an atmospheric glow, while light thrown up through skylights can illuminate planting.

If you do not have a terrace, an arbour overhung by a vine or a similar canopy can provide a spontaneous area for entertaining when a table is positioned beneath. Lit by spotlights concealed in the foliage, it will bathe guests in a soft glow. In the event of a barbecue, the burning embers of charcoal will add their own warm, localized light. These lighting effects in a small garden can be doubled with the imaginative use of mirrors, even creating the impression of another garden beyond.

Subtle focus lighting can make the smallest garden look spectacular. Simply lighting a few carefully chosen features will provide visual signposts that lead the way through the garden. In a very small space, uplighting a statue at the furthest point can be sufficient to add a touch of drama. Outdoor focus lighting falls into two categories: soft features, such as a small tree or shrub, and structural elements, such as a sundial or water feature (see also chapter 11). As with interior lighting, the key is first to determine which items are to be lit and then to conceal the light source so that you see only the effect and not the fitting. Consider what the main viewing angle will be, whether from a window inside or a terrace outside.

Different methods of lighting are required for soft and structural features. With soft features, lighting techniques will differ according to the size, colour and location of the planting.

Seasonal changes also need to be considered as deciduous plants will take on a different appearance from winter to summer, while the textural quality of tree bark provides a strong vertical accent that can be illuminated to great effect all year round. Flowers, highlighted as they come into bloom, provide a brilliant focal point and should be lit with tungsten halogen bulbs, as their white light brings out the true colour of plants. Small trees, such as topiaries, stand out in striking silhouette when the wall behind is lit, either from above or below.

With structural features, a small spiked spotlight, concealed by low-level foliage, will create just the right level of light. If a sundial or urn is positioned in the centre of a grassed area, a fully recessed and adjustable uplighter will provide a discreet solution and will create fewer problems when mowing. Uplighting a trellis can create wonderful effects, not only by illuminating the foliage that may grow up it, but also by accentuating the structural design. A diamond-shaped trellis, for example, creates a strong diagonal pattern with each horizontal element highlighted. Light on foliage will help soften this architectural focus. Planters can be lit by low-voltage fittings, discreetly hidden behind pots and containers due to their small size. The choice of narrow and wide bulbs gives them great versatility. Neon, which is effective when introducing colour and creates a soft upward glow, can also be used at low level to

define a planter. Located below a frosted glass panel with the planter positioned on top, the coloured light will emphasize the shape of the planter, rather than the planting. A white light will create a gentler, less theatrical effect.

Inspirational ideas can become a reality with careful planning. Your long-term vision for the garden will need to be considered and it is essential to look to the future: plants will grow, views will change from season to season and year to year. Low-voltage fittings, mounted on a spike that can be inserted into the ground, allow more flexibility than mains-voltage fixtures and can be moved as the planting changes throughout the seasons. Mains-voltage fixtures need to be hard-wired and if they have to be installed prior to planting, it is difficult to ensure that foliage will be lit properly.

Installing exterior lighting is more costly than installing lights inside the home. If you are completely redesigning your garden and starting from scratch, then installing lights at this stage is much easier, as some excavation work is normally required. The cable to the fittings should be specially armoured or carried within a conduit to ensure it is sealed. It should be buried to a depth that will ensure it remains underground during the normal digging-over of the garden. All connections need to be in waterproof housings, and breakers must be fitted so the power is cut off if any water should

get into the system. Each country or region has its own safety rules and regulations. Wiring should be undertaken by a qualified electrician.

If your garden is already established, the best time for wiring is probably the autumn or spring, to ensure there will be as little damage as possible to the planting. Trunking (the housing for electrical cables), together with any necessary transformers, can be attached at low level to the perimeter walls, concealed by plants. Low-voltage fixtures can be offset from the transformers on long cables. Planning your

lighting in this way will enable you to work around the garden you have already created.

It is helpful to make a sketch when thinking about the lighting design for a garden. As with the interior, where you might choose a favourite painting to form a focal point, you will need to decide which are your most eye-catching plants and create a hierarchy of emphasis. Elements that are to be given more importance and that will need to be specifically lit can be put on one lighting circuit. If you desire a soft wash on the shrubbery in between,

you can put this type of lighting on a separate circuit. Or you might like to consider having structural focal points on a separate circuit so that in winter, when flowers are no longer in bloom, a sundial, urn or perhaps an evergreen tree can be lit to add interest, while allowing bare branches and shrubs to fall into darkness. By organizing your lighting in this way, you can create a harmonious balance.

The atmosphere in a garden can be adjusted according to your mood by raising or lowering light levels. In the early evening the lighting in a

Starlight lanterns, hanging in the branches of a tree, add a decorative touch to a small garden. Spotlights graze up perimeter trees for depth and focus, while miniature floodlights provide a low-level wash of light to the flowerbed.

Caption to be written for this
picture. It can brief and to the
but still lyrical.

A spiked uplighter catching a rose in a garden can make it appear jewel-like.

In addition to the standard uplighter below a tree, simple starlighter lanterns on its branches provide added interest. These small cylinders are perforated and so project pinspot patterns of light among the foliage.

garden is less noticeable but becomes increasingly effective as night falls, so levels of daylight will help to provide a change of mood naturally. But with careful planning and by arranging the lighting on different circuits, the light levels in a garden can be orchestrated from one extreme to another; from a small subtle pool of light immediately outside the house, which prevents a feeling of blackness beyond, to lighting the full garden when entertaining.

Exterior lighting can be controlled by means of a simple switch. In most cases, it should be linked to a photocell to ensure that the lights do not operate during the day; external lighting can go unnoticed until nightfall, which wastes energy. A time clock ensures that the lights are switched off automatically at, say, midnight. With a more extensive lighting scheme, a dimmer system (similar to those used internally) would be more appropriate.

Having decided which techniques to use for general, task and feature lighting, choose light fixtures in the style of the garden. You will need to decide where your fixing points will be and

A statue can be uplit from a spiked spotlight concealed in a planter below. The effect is softened as the uplight filters through the leaves of shrubs, presenting a dappled pattern of light and shadow.

if you require power points on the terrace. A garden is viewed from within as well as from without. For a conservatory, or indeed any room with large windows, lighting the garden is particularly important. At night windows appear black and act like mirrors, reflecting everything within the room, which can result in the feeling of being somewhat exposed. Lighting the garden makes a conservatory a much more comfortable place in which to sit at night, as your eye is drawn through the glass to the brighter planting beyond, and the windows lose their reflective appearance. The lighting within the room should be slightly dimmed so that the light outside appears brighter. With a fully glazed roof, a stretched wire system is preferable to tracks for feature lighting, as it is virtually transparent by day. Wall lights and table lamps can provide local task lighting. With the right balance both inside and out, lighting can provide an infinitely more appealing solution than curtains or blinds.

Outdoor spaces by night can reveal a whole new dimension when given the added sparkle of light. Using the same guidelines as for interiors, we can create drama by highlighting special features, we can provide atmosphere for dining al fresco, balanced by soft general lighting that will make the garden a place to be enjoyed both by day and by night. Do not be afraid to experiment. With the technology now available, garden lighting has never been more flexible – or more creative.

Uplight shining through bamboo forms an attractive backdrop to a small seating area on a roof terrace. The foliage of bamboo is particularly successful when uplit, as its open nature creates lace-like patterns on the surface behind and soft light is reflected from the underside of its leaves. To the left, discreet low-voltage spotlights, fitted with glare cowls, provide a contrasting downlight effect, which emphasizes the timber deck and decorative pebbles.

Recessed, fully sealed fluorescent fixtures, wrapped in magenta gel, can transform a white plastered surface by painting it with coloured light (left). The pink glow contrasts with the crisp white light from low-voltage spotlights that highlight the box hedges. Neatly concealed within planters, they act as crosslights, which increases the drama and heightens the three-dimensional effect.

Recessed floorwashers located between terracotta pots (right) give a soft backlit effect to the grasses and a wash of light to the stone paving. The pots conceal the light source, which in turn produces pleasing patterns of light and shadow.

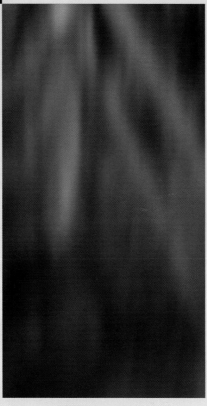

A LARGE GARDEN
PROVIDES DRAMATIC
SCOPE FOR IMAGINATIVE
LIGHTING DESIGNS,
ESPECIALLY WHEN
REFLECTED IN WATER.
TREES CREATE FOCAL
POINTS BOTH IN
SUMMER, WHEN THEIR
LEAFY CANOPIES ARE
LIT, AND IN WINTER,
WHEN BARE BRANCHES
TAKE ON A SCULPTURAL
DIMENSION.

chapter 9

large town and country gardens

In a large town or country garden, exterior lighting comes into its own with a panoply of subtle effects that will enable the garden to look its best. Replicating the appearance of dappled moonlight or uplighting the leafy canopy of an ancient oak, a well-designed lighting scheme can define the structure of a landscape, lend depth and perspective, highlight key focal points and help the garden to fulfil its potential.

As in small gardens, the best landscape lighting is achieved by determining the features in a garden, those elements that are deserving of special attention by means of light. This might be a soft feature, such as a tree or shrub, or a structural feature such as a pergola, statue, temple or water feature. The key to success is to conceal the light source so that only the effect is seen. The principal consideration with a large garden, however, is knowing when to stop. Should you light the whole garden, or small elements within it, such as the terrace and perhaps a tree beyond? This is a matter of personal taste. Above all, consider how the garden will be used and what the various viewing points will be: from the house, within the garden itself, and then perhaps looking back to the house.

Location, too, will have a bearing on how a garden is lit. In northern latitudes, we are more likely to use a large garden in summer, when it gets dark later in the evening. A lighting scheme therefore needs to complement activities such as al fresco dinner parties and perhaps an evening stroll through the garden. In warmer climates it gets dark earlier in summer and the whole expanse of the garden can be used for longer. A lighting scheme needs to take this into consideration. In the country, it is as important to be aware of what not to light, perhaps concentrating on an avenue or terrace and allowing the view of fields and parkland to fade into darkness. Be strategic about how much you light. Light pollution is killing our views of starlit skies, so outside lighting needs to be skilfully thought through and controlled in order to limit light spillage and avoid wasting energy.

In a large garden you are likely to have seating areas located in different parts of the garden so as to take full advantage of its many attractions – perhaps by a lake, or within a folly. A pergola covering a walkway leading to a feature could be lit to create a strong visual focus. With a table and chairs positioned beneath, the seating area becomes the focal point. The pergola itself

can be uplit to highlight its form, as well as lighting a tangle of climbing roses or scented honeysuckle that may form the canopy above. A small spotlight concealed at high level could be directed either across or down to shine onto the table. Combined up/downlighters provide a multi-functional design; when mounted halfway up a pergola they can be used to create more structural definition and uplight a canopy of foliage and downlight a path. Fibre optics, too, can be used in this context, positioned like stars beneath a canopy or pergola.

Lighting a summerhouse or folly at the end of a garden can create a picturesque environment for evening entertaining. Portable lighting effects, such as table or standard lamps, can supplement base lighting to create the feeling of a room outside. It is worth remembering to include sockets for temporary lighting wherever you may need outdoor seating. In addition, a lit garden provides a subtle focus when seen from a distance. The technique of offset lighting, the term used when a structure is lit from afar, works well in large gardens; not only does it illuminate elements at the furthest perimeters and create focus, but it also provides a feeling of extended space. An avenue or vista

leading to a folly is given greater emphasis in this way and the layout of the garden is given greater definition.

Sweeping lawns are often a feature of large gardens and rarely receive the lighting attention they deserve. Lawns can achieve heightened interest when lit by narrow beams from high-level floodlights or by spotlights that are directed to streak across the surface. In winter, lawns are sometimes the only source of colour in a garden, and when lit in this way they can provide both graphic definition and a relief from wintry hues. This effect works best when viewed from one direction, and is especially effective in winter when seen from inside. It is less successful in summer when viewed from within the garden, as the lights can cause glare.

Water is an attractive feature in any garden, but when viewed on a large scale, perhaps in the form of fountains, swimming pools or lakes, subtle use of lighting can maximize its reflective qualities to magnificent effect (see chapter 11).

Plants and trees, however, tend to be the main focus in large landscaped gardens and require a little forward planning. Constantly growing and ever changing, they create different vistas throughout the year. The lighting therefore needs to be flexible to change with the seasons. Certain outdoor fittings come with a spike

attached, which can easily be inserted into the ground. These provide the easiest solution, as they can be moved and adjusted accordingly, whether simply uplighting summer foliage from the front or silhouetting a winter shape from behind. Low-level shrubbery is useful to conceal spiked light fixtures, as it will still allow the light through as long as it is pruned regularly around each light fixture. Light can be dazzling outdoors due to the contrast with the surrounding darkness, so it is always advisable to use a fixture with a glare control, such as a baffle or cowl, so that the bulb is concealed.

If the foliage is dense, with low planting to the front, a general flood of light will work best. Miniature flood fixtures, fitted with shutters known as 'barn door' attachments, are discreet and can be used to direct light exactly where it is required. If the plants themselves have large, dense leaves, they will restrict the path of light and create hot spots, so an alternative solution might be offset lighting, where the light source is remote from the object and floods it from a distance. For small trees or feathery bushes, a spiked spotlight may be more appropriate than a floodlight. When located below the tree or bush, it acts as a subtle uplighter, shining through the leaves. In a formal garden, a box hedge looks elegant if lit with an offset spotlight, which will define its geometric shape. Putting it into silhouette is another effective treatment. Trees make spectacular features when properly lit, their canopies illuminated by uplighters from below. For large trees, a powerful light source, such as sodium, provides a yellow autumnal effect, spectacular when used on a copper beech, while a metal halide will deliver a pure white light which is particularly beautiful for illuminating silver birch, spruce, pines, conifers or cedar trees. It is normally sufficient simply to uplight trees from below. If they are growing in a lawn, a fully buried uplighter is probably the best solution. If a tree is set in planting or woodland, a spiked fitting will stand above the low ground cover and is less likely to become overgrown and concealed. An alternative would be to use an elastic tree strap to tie the light fixture to the trunk just above foliage level. As the tree grows, the elastic strap allows for expansion, although in time, depending on the rate of growth, it will need to be replaced. In some cases, a light fitting can be located to catch the front of the tree canopy by projecting light at an angle from a distance. Again, it is important to look at the viewing angles to ensure that the effect does not create glare. For large trees, two lights may be required: a narrow beam, positioned close to the trunk, and a medium beam, slightly offset to catch the canopy of the tree.

With the appropriate lighting techniques, moonlight can be yours every night of the year. While this effect can be created effectively in smaller gardens, too (see page 143), when used

for trees with a large canopy this can be spectacular. By placing metal halide bulbs with narrow to medium downward reflectors high in the trees, light can be directed downwards through the foliage to provide dappled moonlit patterns on the ground below. Just imagine this type of lighting illuminating an avenue. It is important that some form of baffle or glare shield is used to prevent a direct view of the source. Invariably the bulbs need to be tilted out to light the canopy fully, and 'barn door' attachments may be necessary. A practical advantage of this method of lighting is that the fixtures are less likely to become overgrown and lost. However, the disadvantages lie in fact that the wiring has to be run up the side of the tree and the fixtures need to be placed as high as possible, making maintenance difficult. The wiring should be as unobtrusive as possible and can be colour-matched to the tree.

A seat, positioned beneath a large tree with metal halide moonlight filtering through its branches, can provide a romantic place to pause at the furthest point of a woodland walk. The cool ambience of this kind of lighting contrasts well with the decorative warmth of incandescent or candle lanterns scattered around a terrace.

Lighting palms and other trees with long trunks and small canopies, such as pines, requires a very narrow-beamed light source that will

graze light up the trunk and provide a soft uplight effect to the leaves. Lighting a line of palms gives a strong processional approach to any entrance. Putting trees into silhouette can be achieved when lighting a wall behind them. In this way the shape and form of the trees will appear as a dramatic outline. In addition, if reflected light is required to help illuminate a pathway, the silhouette option is a practical solution.

Most light fittings for the garden are black, but the neatest are those finished in dark green, which blend in with the colour of garden foliage. Copper fixtures can be effective, as they will wear to a pleasing green patina with age. Bronze-coloured fittings are also suitable, particularly if they are mounted in a tree, as their natural colour blends in with the colour of the trunk.

With large gardens, in either town or country, the scope for lighting is amplified, but the most magical results are often achieved with minimal light fixtures. In gardens, less is usually more where lighting is concerned and by subtle use of techniques a garden can be revealed in a whole new light. From moonlit tree canopies overhead and lush summer foliage, lit from below, to bold silhouettes of palm trees and cross-lit swathes of lawn, all these effects are now possible through the medium of light.

Recessed uplighters emphasize the interior of a pergola, catching the planting that provides an almost solid canopy overhead. This form of lighting gives a soft reflected light to the table, which is supplemented by candles in storm lanterns, making the perfect location for a summer supper party.

Creating focus is as important for exteriors as it is for interiors, and a series of lighting effects can build focus around a special feature. A fountain is crosslit from within the pool. Cypress trees are uplit from small spiked fixtures to either side, providing a perfect frame to the fountain, while in the foreground miniature fibre-optic steplights are used to light each step.

A Spanish mirador, viewed across a pool, is a stunning example of how a building can be read in silhouette (above).
A lantern lights the top section and a soft uplighter, located behind the seating, lights the lower section (right).
Combined with candlelight, the perfect mood is set. The whole effect is mirrored softly in the adjoining pool, the
water jets ensuring a continuous ripple so that the reflection is attractively blurred.

A view is framed with flowers by day and with light by night (left). A soft, low-voltage uplighter, spiked into the ground below, lights the timber column and the planting, bringing out the deep purple of the blossoms against the night sky.

An ancient olive tree can be as spectacular as a piece of sculpture when lit at night (left). When crosslit from below by two spiked uplighters, its shape and form are emphasized. The planting beneath the tree helps to conceal the light sources, so that the effect alone can be appreciated.

OVERLEAF

Tall palm trees require a very narrow beam of light to highlight their trunks and the small canopy above. This is best achieved with narrow 4-degree spotlights, which can be fully recessed into a lawn or spiked into low planting. When the wind blows, a wonderful diffused light effect is created.

Scotch pines appear to float
between two columns when lit with
a metal halide source, which
emphasizes the blue tones of the
trees (above). Wide-beamed spiked
fittings have been used, positioned
so that they emerge above the low
planting to create maximum effect.
When viewed from below (left), a
filigree pattern is the result.

IT IS THE ENTRANCE
THAT SETS THE SCENE
AND CREATES THE
FIRST IMPRESSION OF
ANY HOME. AS SUCH,
IT SHOULD BE
WELCOMING AS WELL
AS BEING IN
CHARACTER WITH ITS
SURROUNDINGS.

entrances and exits

A well-lit, entrance should provide a welcoming reception, enhance the architecture and adjacent borders or terraces and create a subtle focus, so that the exterior can look as effective by night as the interior. Exits are just as important, ensuring smooth progress from house to garden. Having enhanced your home both inside and outside with light, entrances, exits and corridors should be treated with equal importance, as they set the scene and help to create mood as well as link different spaces.

With a large house, the first view may be that of the gateway at the beginning of a drive. This can be highlighted by using recessed uplighters, which will just graze the posts to either side and can be more effective than a traditional lantern. If the posts are uplit from both sides, you will create the same pleasing effect on leaving as on arriving. Uplighters can also be used to light any decorative features, such as an urn, that may complement a gateway or flank a drive.

For most houses, it is the front door that creates the first impression. You may wish to make a striking impact or you may prefer a more subtle approach. In either event, an entrance should be inviting. It also sets the scene, making a visual statement that hints at what lies within. Lighting that conveys a sense of cool, geometric precision would be fitting for a contemporary glass-and-steel house, but a warm wash of light over the door and surrounding mellow brickwork would be appropriate to an older style of house.

The doorway forms the principal focus of any façade, both visually and practically, and deserves special attention. The traditional approach would be to locate a hanging lantern in the porch or a decorative wall lantern on either one, or both, sides of the doorway. A more contemporary idea is to use a modern wall light on either side. A combined up/downlighter, for example, will create a dramatic pool of light both upwards and downwards, accentuating architectural details or putting any planting in pots into silhouette. This device can help to improve the proportions of an entrance, making it appear larger or wider. Standard uplighters can be used to similar effect. Alternatively, a small downlighter, recessed into a projecting canopy or porch, will graze down a front door, providing a pool of light to the threshold. This looks effective when viewed from a distance, but is not particularly comfortable to stand under. By adding wall lights, one to each side, the effect is softened.

Lights located by a front door are often best controlled by a PIR (passive infra-red detector) so that they operate only during darkness and come on for a short period of time when someone approaches. This can also be used as a security device. With an override switch, the lights can remain on all evening if required, without continually flashing on and off.

An entrance needs to be considered in the context of both the surrounding architecture and the setting. All successful lighting arrangements, whether interior or exterior, need to be in sympathy with the style of the house, and different buildings require different lighting techniques. Dramatic emphasis can be given to an entrance simply by floodlighting the front of a house, providing it is set back from the road. This can look very effective but tends to flatten architectural modelling and can cause glare when viewed from inside. Low-level mood lighting around the base of a building, on the other hand, adds reflected light to the surroundings and helps to light pathways. Spiked uplighters through foliage, or small uplights recessed into gravel, create a subtle effect. A more selective lighting scheme, in which individual features are accentuated, can produce eye-catching effects. Elevations with detailed

A traditional portico with a low ceiling has insufficient height for a formal lantern (below). Two discreet low-voltage downlighters are the perfect solution, lighting the doorway, putting the columns into silhouette and creating focus.

decoration, or special features such as arches, columns or an entrance portico, can be highlighted by means of recessed fittings. Pilasters along a façade are most dramatically lit using narrow-beam recessed uplighters set at ground level. In some instances, flowerbeds can be used to conceal uplighters, allowing the light to filter through planting or creepers and creating dappled light and shade on the side of the house. This random approach creates a less formal and more magical effect. The window architraves of an elaborate stone building can be discreetly lit by placing light fittings directly in front of the window on the sill. By manipulating the light source and avoiding glare (by means of a spreader lens and glare grille), an elongated beam will light the architrave effectively. A flat-fronted Georgian building will look its best when lit with a soft wash of light, while a more contemporary exterior, comprised largely of glass, may receive sufficient lighting from within.

If your home is in a town or city with streetlights, it will require stronger light sources to create an impact. In the country, moonlight may occasionally be enough to guide the way, but a little extra light will still be required to highlight an entrance. A tungsten halogen light source provides the truest colour rendering and can be used on the exterior of most houses, unless the building is particularly large when a warmer light source, such as sodium, is preferable. Metal halide is a cool light source and is best employed for city applications where a clean, white light appears more dramatic. If used in the country it can seem a little cold and unwelcoming.

Just as entrances prepare us for the interiors to come, so exits should facilitate a calm shift into the garden beyond. Areas immediately outside French windows, such as terraces, require good lighting, not only for practical reasons but also to provide a gentle transition between house and garden. If lights are too bright inside, reflections on the glazing will kill the effect of lighting in the garden, so it is important to be able to control lighting close to an exit or windows onto a terrace. By softening these lights with a dimmer, you can heighten the intensity of the lighting outside.

Pathways can be integrated as part of the overall design with well-planned lighting. Paths need to be illuminated for practical reasons, to provide safe and easy access from house to garden or from one part of the garden to another. But this kind of lighting can be just as decorative as that in other parts of the garden. Sometimes reflected light from lit features, such as planting or a statue, is adequate to light a route, but special attention should be given to changes in levels. Decorative local indicator lights can be provided by LEDs or light-emitting diodes), which are effective

when used to delineate a route or when set beneath a handrail. LEDs, commonly used in digital watches and pocket calculators, provide a very low-heat light source, which makes them appropriate in this context. They can form part of a pattern within paving by replacing a tile detail with the light source, and, with their long bulb life, LEDs can also be an alternative miniature light source to fibre optics. There is no remote light box to conceal, just a small transformer. They perform best as indicator lights but are not ideal at projecting light for any distance. Choose the light source most appropriate for your needs.

If there are walls on either side of a flight of steps, a bricklight (so called because its size and shape are exactly the same as a brick) could be recessed into the wall to provide a general wash of light across the steps. This fitting, seen more in commercial applications, works well in the context of a private home as long as it has a louvre covering it to direct the light downwards. For a dramatic effect, directional spotlights can be set into the wall to light each step individually. Fibre optics, with their miniaturized fixtures, are ideal in this situation. If there are only a few stone steps, it may be possible to conceal a continuous low-voltage strip under the front nosing of the steps to provide a continuous downward wash of light. This works well only if the light source is hidden; otherwise the

effect is too glitzy and gives the impression of approaching a hotel.

The same principles apply to lighting paths and steps in gardens large and small, but there are additional possibilities that work well on a large scale. A small spotlight, located in a tree and directed downwards, can provide sufficient dappled light to illuminate a path possibly in a woodland setting. If localized light is required, this could be in the form of a small copper mushroom-style fixture or a bollard light, some types of which can be integrated into stone boulders. Gas torchères can be fitted to create a pathway of flickering light, which provides a touch of theatre for special occasions.

Entrances, exits and the paths that link the spaces in between need to be well lit for purely functional reasons. But there are aesthetic benefits, too. During daylight, windows provide a visual link between the rooms of a house and the garden beyond. Sympathetic exterior lighting at night can help re-establish the idea of the garden as an extension of the home, while enhancing architectural nuances and revealing surface textures which may not be apparent by day. Whether your home is old or new, a successful lighting scheme is all about establishing harmony between a building and its surroundings, which can intrigue as much during the hours of darkness as by daylight.

As the evening progresses from
dusk to late evening, lighting
becomes more predominant and the
contrast of effects more dramatic
(above and right). Low-level
recessed bricklights emphasize the
steps in the foreground, recessed
uplighters at either side of the plant
pots uplight the small standard
trees, while spiked lights close to the
house shine up through foliage to
bring out the texture of
the stonework.

A frame of light is created around
the exit into a garden (left) by
combination up/down wall lights.
These provide the right level of
light to ensure a smooth path from
inside to outside.

Looking back towards the house
from the garden (below), an
archway of foliage is softly uplit by
concealed spiked lights. The house
itself is illuminated by recessed
low-voltage uplighters that graze
the brickwork and frame the
welcoming glow within.

Down a garden path, small highlights are created by low-voltage sources that glance across the decking, reflecting off the grasses on the opposite side. Recessed uplighters at the base of the espaliered trees create a focus at eye level, while in the distance the rear terrace is emphasized by spotlights concealed beneath the bench, which create streaks of light across the paving.

A weeping pear tree, framed by an archway, becomes the focus of attention at the end of a path when lit by a narrow-beam super spotlight, located high up in a tree some 6 metres (18 feet) above. The foliage to either side is softly lit by concealed spiked light fixtures, which can be moved as the seasons change, while the path receives a gentle, indirect light from both sources.

LIGHT, COLOUR AND
WATER, USED IN
COMBINATION, CAN
TURN AN ORDINARY
GARDEN INTO
SOMETHING EXTRA-
ORDINARY. FIBRE OPTICS
FLOOD WALLS WITH ANY
COLOUR IN THE
SPECTRUM, CINEMATIC
PATTERNS CAN BE
PROJECTED ONTO
SURFACES AND WATER
RILLS BECOME A RIBBON
OF LIGHT.

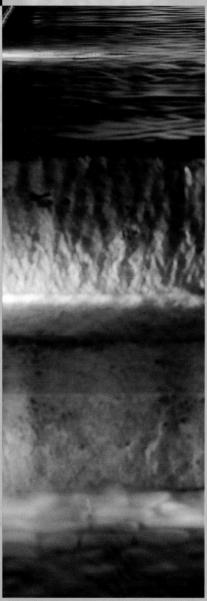

chapter 11

special features

For a special occasion, any outdoor space, from the tiniest roof terrace to rolling acres, can be transformed with light – and a little bit of imagination. Lighting can provide a spectacular backdrop for indulgent entertaining on a grand scale or a small gathering of friends. You could celebrate Midsummer's Eve with a romantically lit picnic or highlight a magical winter landscape for Christmas. Any event that requires a touch of theatre or sheer glamour can become a night to remember. Accent lighting can turn special features into visual statements; floodlighting introduces a sense of spectacle; colour brings another dimension to a lighting display, while candles can create a spell-binding scene. Water is perhaps the most bewitching special effect of all. By incorporating into your outdoor lighting scheme some of the effects that follow, you can turn your vision into a reality.

Focus lighting for structural features, such as a statue, or for soft features, such as topiary, can be used for special occasions to create a sense of added mystery and drama. A sculpture or urn can be a striking focus, especially when pale stone is contrasted against a dark hedge. A small concealed halogen light located in front of the object will provide an even light. Statues can

also be lit using a spiked spotlight concealed by foliage. Topiary, perhaps flanking an entrance or exit, looks effective when put into silhouette by downlighting from above and highlighting the base with small low-voltage spiked lights.

For theatre on a grand scale, floodlighting can be used. Castles and great houses often benefit from this effect, bathed in a warm, golden sodium light. Mercury light sources produce a distinctly blue light, which is particularly effective on evergreens and contrasts well with tungsten lights used elsewhere. Floodlights can be sunk in the ground and if located in a clump of trees, this will help to avoid glare. Otherwise floodlighting is best reserved for dense areas of foliage or for distant corners.

The flickering light of candles creates a wonderful impression at night, and it is the simplest of effects to achieve. A functional pathway can become spectacular at night when flanked by flaring garden torches; nightlights can be floated on water while candles in storm glasses, either grouped or used alone, light steps or mark the boundary of a terrace or seating area. (Remember that flames should never be left unattended and should always be kept away from foliage and overhanging branches.)

Water brings depth and mystery to a garden – even the simplest waterspout has expressive qualities – but it is light that brings it to life. Water can be contained in a variety of different ways, many of which derive from past traditions. The paradise gardens of Islam were designed around the four rivers of life, later to be translated into the channels, basins, jets and water courtyards of the great gardens of the Alhambra in Granada. In the hills of Kashmir these traditions were transformed into tumbling chutes or *chadars*, faceted to catch the natural light and to amplify the sound of falling water. For sheer exuberance, nothing can match the gardens of the Italian Renaissance and their magnificent fountains and cascades, while the water gardens of Japan are designed for quiet contemplation.

These examples can provide inspiration for our own designs. New materials and modern technology allow us to control and contain water in almost any form: as formal, geometric pools or organic, natural designs; as still, reflective pools or moving spouts. Water can flow through and across paving or fill canals and rills. It can be introduced into the smallest garden and is especially welcome in urban spaces, its reflected light counteracting the oppression of high walls or tall enclosing buildings while the sound of trickling water can help to muffle the noise of traffic.

Water and light make a dynamic partnership, especially when water is animated, whether arched in jets or falling in cascades. When lighting waterspouts, submerged narrow-beam sources set at the base of each jet will uplight the water, making it sparkle magnificently. A low-voltage source can be used, or alternatively small fibre optics can be located within the spout of water itself. With a bubble jet, where the water spout is low, the effect is almost like that of small candles floating on the surface, as the water tends to hold the light. If a higher jet is required for a fountain, the light source should be located beside the jet rather than within the spout, so that light illuminates the entire length of the water spray. For low-voltage fittings a suitable position needs to be found for the transformer, which can often be located by the pump, while intelligent transformers can now be located remotely as they compensate for voltage drop. For fibre optics, however, the light box needs to be located as close as possible to the fittings. Each case needs to be considered individually.

Waterfalls come in many forms, from minimalist cascades to more natural designs, creating thin translucent curtains or tumbling falls of water. The most dramatic effects are achieved when

the light is literally under the fall of the water. Careful positioning of spotlights, set at various points among the rocks, is necessary to ensure that the water itself appears to be illuminated. Flexibility should be built into the design to maximize the impact. If the lights are on long cables, positioning can be left to the end of the installation when the exact fall of water has been determined. The lights can be located discreetly among loose rocks.

Water rills, similar in style to those that link the terraces of the Alhambra, can glitter with imaginative lighting. Usually rills take the form of shallow steps of water that link one pool to another. When lit with fibre optics incorporated at either side, each step appears to be illuminated, giving the impression of a spectacular ribbon of light. The colour of the light can be enhanced by the choice of base for the rill. A mellow stone rill, for example, will result in an almost golden glow. Another approach to a narrow, straight rill might be to light it using a continuous concealed source on either side (where the rill has a flat base, a more even ribbon of light will be achieved). Pebbles arranged along the base will produce a pleasing pattern of light and shadow.

Still water, in the manner of the Japanese-style pool, creates a different mood in a garden. Reflective as glass, it provides a sanctuary for quiet contemplation. It also has different

lighting requirements. When lighting water features, the best effects are achieved when the water is clear, and this occurs either when there is movement or where there is no plant growth. In a still pond with plant growth, underwater lighting can be a mistake, as it will merely highlight murky depths. In this instance, it is best to leave the water unlit as a reflective surface. Still and flat by day, it will reflect the moving sky above; by night it has a mirror-like sheen. Any nearby feature that is lit will be reflected within the pool, and this in itself can be magical. A still pool can be enhanced with the addition of a lit sculpture, which can be traditional and figurative or modern and abstract, depending on the style of its setting. Uplit with underwater spotlights, or crosslit with illumination from the banks on either side, a sculpture can provide a stunning focal point. The curved ellipse of a bowl, silhouetted at the end of a reflective pool and lit from within by means of a gas torchère, would be equally spectacular.

The shimmering blue depths of a swimming pool can look stunning at night, creating a strong visual focus and providing an element of general light. For really effective lighting, the light sources need to be set into the sides of the pool below the surface of the water, creating subtle areas of light and shadow. Low-voltage light sources are ideal for pool lighting, in particular the smaller, more powerful halogen

An urn with swan features at the corners is highlighted from its base by four miniature fibre optic light sources. A further source is incorporated within the spout of water itself, resulting in a lit bubble jet that glows like a night light. In the distance, foliage is lit with low-voltage spiked lights that can be adjusted as the plants grow.

lights, which are discreet in appearance. Fibre optics are another possibility, depending on the effect you wish to create. Their tiny points of light create a sparkling effect when recessed into a pattern at the base of a pool, used to illuminate steps, or set into the edge of the pool delineating its perimeter with light. If a colour wheel is introduced at the light source, this will create the opportunity for changing colours, ideal for special occasions.

Water is one of the most exciting subjects for garden lighting, but there are yet more possibilities when creating special features in the garden. As a means of linking spaces, or breaking up an area into different 'rooms' or compartments, a bridge acts as a design device in a larger garden. When properly lit, however, it becomes not only functional but also a magical visual focus – imagine twinkling lights, positioned like stars beneath the archway. Fibre optics are the perfect solution when used in this context. As paths over water, the potential for special effects on bridges is amplified. Uplit with underwater lighting, a bridge's structure will be dramatically highlighted. Illuminated from the banks on either side, it will be singled out as a key element in a garden (this effect is best viewed from afar as glare can occur if viewed close-up). Local indicator lights in the form of LEDs, installed at ground level or set beneath a handrail to delineate the pathway, are both functional and decorative. Mirrored in the

Recessed uplighters are an essential lighting tool in any garden. Lights set into a timber deck have been fitted with a red filter to colour the plain, plastered wall. This contrasts with the cool green of the swimming pool. Coloured filters offer an infinite palette that can be changed to suit the occasion. What is austerely white by day can be transformed with colour by night.

reflective water beneath, these lighting effects create twice the impact. Your choice of lighting should be determined by the style of bridge, ancient or modern. Recessed uplighters work well with a traditional stone bridge, emphasizing architectural elements such as pilasters, while lights recessed into side walls will wash across the path. Lighting with coloured LEDs is more sympathetic to contemporary design.

For a special occasion, coloured light can lend a sense of theatre but should be used selectively. Coloured glass filters on recessed uplighters, fitted with a cool, white light source, will wash a white wall with soft colour (if the wall is brick the coloured effect will be less successful). It is visually exciting to explore the cooler blue-green end of the spectrum, while a palette of reds and yellows on a light stucco wall will create contrast to the green of the garden. On a light-coloured terrace, some pinks or yellows may be acceptable, though there is the danger of creating a discotheque look. Alternatively, think of linking your exterior colour to that of the adjacent room inside for a sense of continuity. As plants and trees have their own inherent colours, coloured light is for the most part unnecessary with planting: white light brings out their true colour best. For a special occasion, though, cool blues and greens can lend extra depth to large trees while a cool blue-white light will give the bewitching effect of moonlight.

Coloured filters can also be used to light water features, using fibre optics fitted with a colour wheel. Stunning examples of light, colour and water, used in combination, can be seen in some of our most beautiful cities, providing inspiration for our own designs. The courtyard at Somerset House in London, for example, contains water jets that appear to spout from cracks in the paving; each jet is surrounded by heads of fibre optics – a number of which can change colour – creating an impressive effect.

Light can become an art form in its own right, and when displayed in a garden by night will create a very special focal point. Imagine a frosted glass screen, illuminated by coloured lights concealed within it. Either the three primary colours of light (red, blue and green) or the three secondary colours (cyan, magenta and yellow) can be installed; by controlling each colour individually and combining colours together, any hue in the spectrum can be achieved. Controlled on a programmed dimmer, the colours can be changed automatically. You could feature a particular colour each night, or the lighting could be set to slowly cross-fade, offering infinite changes throughout the evening.

An alternative to a red filter might be a soft lilac – another colour, another mood (above). For a fixed installation, a low-voltage uplighter will need to be replaced by fibre optic uplighters and a colour wheel. To create a temporary pathway of coloured light for a special occasion, a colour filter can simply be laid (for a short time only) on top of the light fitting.

Coloured lighting is not advisable with brickwork; instead, white light will bring out its inherent colour and texture (right).

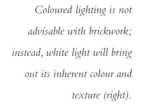

Lighting can even create the impression of ever-changing spaces and vistas. A back wall that catches sunlight during the day will create a totally different impression at night if colourful slides of images or pattern are projected onto it. Any number of subjects work in this capacity: a soft wave pattern, an abstract painting, or an escapist landscape. Again, the images can be made to change during the evening, or each night. In a contemporary garden, a series of vertical white panels of stretched canvas, used to reflect light during the daytime, make perfect projector screens after dark, creating cinematic after-dinner entertainment.

By day a garden can appear elegant or informal, an essay in urban minimalism or a lush wilderness. But by night, it can become a captivating light show. Whether you choose to light water features or play with coloured light, manipulate accent lighting or floodlighting, when special effects are called for and a touch of theatre, light takes centre stage.

Light projections can transform a white, reflective surface during the day into a piece of art at night. An undulating wave pattern, coloured by a blue filter, decorates a plain wall (above). The cool metal halide light source is concealed beneath the underside of the balcony (right).

The shallow steps of a water rill are emphasized by incorporating fibre optics at each change in level (left). They catch the running water and reflect off the opposite side, creating a golden ribbon of light. The pathways that descend alongside the water chute are lit by miniature low-voltage floods, hidden in the planting on either side.

Fibre optic light sources lead the eye to an urn, which is in turn discreetly lit by a fibre optic light in each corner (right and above). Light boxes are located within 10 metres (30 feet) in manholes, sunk into the surrounding stone paving.

PREVIOUS PAGES
A detail of a pool light, shining through a water jet, illustrates how light is attracted to any sort of air bubble and creates wonderful abstract patterns (left).

The mystique of a horse rising up out of the water is achieved by lighting the sculpture with intensely focused fibre optics, located at the base of the pool (right). The flickering light moves as the water moves and the horse appears almost to tense its muscles with the action of the light. Candles set in Moroccan lanterns help to reinforce the exotic ambience.

glossary

Baffle
Device attached to a light fitting that helps to prevent glare. The source of light is set back behind a tube to conceal it.

Ballast
Adapts characteristics of the electrical supply to suit the lamp; normally used with fluorescent tubes or metal halide light sources.

Barn-door attachment
Device originally used in the theatre; it has four shutters that can be adjusted to frame the light.

Beam widths
The cone of light produced by a reflector can vary. A narrow beam could have a 10-degree angle, a medium beam a 25-degree angle and a wide beam 40-degree.

Bollard light
Low-level post light, which has a similar purpose to a path light but is tougher and sturdier. Frequently used in commercial situations.

Bricklight
Light roughly the size of a brick, usually used at low level for steps.

Bulbs
The means by which fittings are illuminated. In the lighting trade, bulbs are called lamps. They take on a variety of effects depending on whether they are clear, frosted, or have an inbuilt diffuser. Incandescent bulbs have a warm light and are normally associated with table lamps; tungsten halogen bulbs have a white light and are more often associated with low-voltage fittings.

Colour saturation
The amount of pure colour in relation to its brightness. For intense colour, use coloured light on a wall of the same colour.

Colour wheel
Wheel with various colours, usually used with fibre optics, which allows for choice of up to six different hues.

Up/downlighter
Wall light that is usually cylindrical and combines spotlights that shine both upwards and downwards.

Control system
System linked to all lighting, which can be manipulated to create special effects, such as scene setting.

Cowl attachment
Attachment to reduce the glare from a fitting.

Dichroic lamp
Bulb that has a reflector designed to pass the majority of its heat output backwards, in the opposite direction to the beam of light.

Dimmer system (also dimmer switch)
Means by which to raise/lower lighting levels, combined with an ability to activate pre-set scenes which set the mood of a room.

End-emitting fibres (see Fibre optics)

Fibre optics
These are created by a single light source, located remotely in what is known as a light box. A special reflector focuses the light down individual glass fibres, usually enveloped in black sheaths, which emit light at their ends. They emit no ultra-violet rays and no heat. If side emitting, they have no black sheath and their entire length is lit.

Filter
Usually of glass, which can be frosted or coloured.

Floodlight
A fitting that creates a wide spread of light; miniature flood fixtures create a similar effect but are much smaller as they use a low-voltage source with wide-beam reflector.

Fluorescent
A cool light source from a slim strip of varying lengths. Can be dimmed if an electronic ballast is used. When dimmed, they become less bright but do not become warmer in colour like a tungsten source.

Footlight fixtures
Small low-voltage fixture usually fitted to the front of a shelf.

Framing projector
A projector that is fully concealed within the ceiling, leaving only a small aperture through which light passes. A technician is required to cut a copper mask so that the beam of light exactly frames paintings or objects.

Gel
As used in the theatre; transparent, heat-resistant plastic used to add colour to a light source.

Glare grille
Attachment used to reduce glare; see also Louvres.

Gobo
A thin metal stencil with a cut-out pattern; when a light source is shone through it an image is projected onto a surface.

Halogen
A gas introduced around a tungsten filament bulb to create a whiter light. It can be mains voltage or low voltage.

Incandescent light (see Bulbs)

Intelligent glass
Description of glass that changes its characteristics when an electric current is passed through it, eg it can change from clear to opaque.

LEDs
Light emitting diodes provide a very low-heat light source with a very long lamp life – around 50,000 hours and are usually red, blue or cool white.

Lens
Accessory used to achieve different effects from the same fitting. A spreader lens creates an elongated beam of light when used in conjunction with a narrow-beam bulb. A softening lens provides a softer wash of light. A frosted lens achieves a more even wash of light. A UV lens removes the ultra violet from a beam and is used particularly with art works to prevent fading and ageing.

Light box (see Fibre optics)

Louvre
An attachment with horizontal or vertical fins, sometimes adjustable. When added to a light fitting it is directional and reduces glare.

Low-voltage
A low-voltage bulb fitting operates at 12 volts rather than the usual mains voltage. The advantage of 12v is that the filament in the lamp can be manufactured to a smaller size, which results in a more discreet light source.

Low-voltage strip (track)
A type of track operating at low voltage into which small bulbs can be slotted along its length, either continuously or at intervals.

Mains voltage
Any bulb that operates at 230v (Europe) or 120v (USA).

Metal halide
Bulb that is often used in commercial floodlighting. Uses a ballast and provides a cooler light, is energy efficient, but cannot easily be dimmed.

Neon
In principle, neon is similar to a customized fluorescent tube. Usually coloured, it can be manufactured to any shape and is often used in signage.

Offset lighting
Term used when lighting a building or wall from a distance.

Photocell
A sensor that monitors daylight and controls lights to go on or off at particular daylight levels.

Pinspot
Narrow focused beam of light.

PIR
Passive infra-red presence detector, which can automatically operate a light.

Pre-set scenes
Combined lighting circuits specifically chosen to achieve a certain mood where a control system is used.

Recessed fitting
Discreet fitting that can be positioned within the ceiling, floor or wall. Always flush with the level of a surface.

Reflectance values
The proportion of incident light that is reflected by a given surface.

Reflected light
Light that is bounced off a wall or object; also used to convey quality of that light.

Reflector
This can form part of a bulb or fitting and is used to direct light in a specific beam. Can be designed to provide either a narrow or wide distribution of light.

Refracted light
Light that changes direction as it passes through glass or water.

Rope lights
A run of small 'pea' bulbs set into a flexible rubber covering. Available as low or mains voltage with a lamp life of around 10,000 hours.

Sodium light
Powerful yellow/orange light source that is used on a grand scale when lighting castles and great houses; also once used in street lighting. It requires a ballast and is very energy efficient. When white sodium (or son) is specified, the colour is more like tungsten and less yellow.

Spiked fittings
Variety of outdoor fittings that come with a spike to be inserted into the ground. As such these fittings are very flexible.

Spill light
Light that goes beyond the object being lit.

Switch lines
The various fittings that are connected to one switch or dimmer. Each circuit has a different switch.

Switch plate
Control for switch lines. This could be a 'dimmer' or an on/off control. A number of different circuits can be controlled from one plate.

Transformer
Device that reduces the domestic electricity supply from mains voltage to the required low voltage. Can be integral to the fitting or remote.

Trunking
Housing for cables.

Tungsten
Tungsten is the filament usually used inside a light bulb that heats up to provide light. The resulting light is warm and inviting, which is effective in the evening but can look insipid during the day.

Wire system
Type of track with two tensioned cables, powered at 12v, carrying current to small low-voltage fittings placed between the cables. The transformer can be at the end of the wires or located remotely as long as it is within 4m (12ft).

credits

Lighting design throughout all properties is either by Lighting Design International or John Cullen Lighting.

Landscape design by **Christopher Bradley-Hole** – pages 22, 149 bottom and 174.

Architecture by **Timothy Hatton Architecture** and interior decoration by **Mlinaric, Henry** and **Zervudachi** – pages 32/33, 36/37, 51, 57, 64, 72/3, 74/5, 97, and 130/1.

Interior design by **Karen Mulville** – pages 38/39, 41, 45, 59, 65, 86/7, 96, 100, 122/3 and 127.

Architecture by **Rolfe Judd** – pages 42/43, 102/3, 128/9 and 146.

Interior design by **Taylor Howes Design Ltd** – pages 52/53, 54/55, 84 top, 132/3 and 134/5.
Interior design by **Alison Henry** – pages 80, 90, 104/5, 106/7, 118/9, 120/1, 155 and 168.

Garden design by **Bartholemew Landscapes** – page 149 top.

Landscape design by **Arabella Lennox-Boyd** – pages 156/157, 158/159, 162/163, 164/165, 179, 185, 186/187 and back jacket.

Designers' contact details:
Bartholemew Landscapes
Tel: 020 7931 8685
Christopher Bradley-Hole
Tel: 020 7727 3320
Timothy Hatton Architecture
Tel: 020 7727 3484

Alison Henry
Tel. 01993 824910
John Cullen Lighting
Tel: 020 7371 5400
Arabella Lennox-Boyd
Tel: 020 7931 9995
Lighting Design International
Tel: 020 7381 8999
Mlinaric, Henry and Zervudachi
Tel: 020 7730 9072
Rolfe Judd
Tel: 020 7556 1500
Taylor Howes Design Ltd
Tel: 020 7349 9017

index

suppliers' directory

Aero
347-349 Kings Road
London SW3 5ES
Tel. 020 7351 0511
www.aeroliving.com
Contemporary European lighting

Aktiva
10b Spring Place
London NW5 3BH
Tel. 020 7428 9325
www.aktiva.co.uk
Low-voltage modern fittings

Ann's
34 a-b Kensington
   Church Street
London W8 4HA
Tel. 020 7937 5033
*Classic chandeliers, lamp bases
and shades*

Aram Store
110 Drury Lane
London WC2B 5SG
Tel. 020 7557 7557
www.aram.co.uk
*Contemporary designs for the
home and office*

Atrium
Centrepoint
22-24 St Giles High St
London WC2H 8TA
Tel. 020 7379 7288
www.atrium.ltd.uk
Contemporary lighting

Babylon
301 Fulham Road
London SW10 9QH
Tel. 020 7376 7255
www.babylonlondon.com
Contemporary lighting

Bella Figura
G5 Chelsea Harbour
   Design Centre
Lots Road
London SW10 0XE
Tel. 020 7376 4564
*Classic and contemporary
lighting*

**Besselink, Jones &
Milne**
99 Walton Street
London SW3 2HH
Tel. 020 7584 0343
www.besselink.com
*Wide range of traditional
lighting designs*

BHS Plc
252-258 Oxford Street
London W1N 9DC
Tel. 020 7629 2011
*Affordable traditional and
modern fittings*

CTO Lighting
35 Park Avenue North
London N8 7RU
Tel. 020 8340 4593
info@cto-lighting.co.uk
www.cto-lighting.co.uk
*Lights for tables, floors, walls
and ceilings in modern materials*

Candela Ltd
47 Abbey Business
   Centre
Ingate Place
London SW8 3NS
Tel. 020 7720 4480
www.candela.ltd.uk
mail@candela.ltd.uk
*Range of low-voltage
downlights*

Comet Lighting
43 Wolborough Street
Newton Abbott
Devon TQ12 1JG
Tel. 01626 332255
*Traditional brass wall, picture
and desk lamps*

The Conran Shop
Michelin House
81 Fulham Road
London SW3 6RD
Tel. 020 7589 7401
www.conran.co.uk
conranshop@dial.pipex.
com
*Excellent range of contemporary
lights*

Creative Element
2 King Lane
Clitheroe
Lancashire BB7 1AA
Tel. 01200 427313
*Contemporary interior design
including lighting*

John Cullen Lighting
585 Kings Road
London SW6 2EH
Tel. 020 7371 5400
www.johncullenlighting.
co.uk
*Discreet lighting for house and
garden; also consultancy service*

Designer Light Shop
4 Kennington Road
London SE1 7BL
Tel. 020 7928 0097
*Stylish European contemporary
lighting*

Donghia
G23 Chelsea Harbour
   Design Centre
London SW10 0XE
Tel. 020 7823 3456
*Modern chandeliers, table and
floor lamps*

Charles Edwards
582 Kings Road
London SW6 2DY
Tel. 020 7736 8490
Charles@charlesedwards
.demon.co.uk
*Reproduction lights from late
18th century onwards*

Hector Finch Lighting
88 Wandsworth Bridge Rd
London SW6 2TF
Tel. 020 7731 8886
hector@hectorfinch.com
Antique light fittings

Pierre Frey
251-253 Fulham Road
London SW3 6HY
Tel. 020 7376 5599
Contact.uk@pierrefrey.
com
*Contemporary table lamps in
crystal, leather and wood*

Gotham
17 Chepstow Corner
1 Pembridge Villas
London W2 4XE
Tel. 020 7243 0011
dvlonergan@aol.com
*A range of lamp styles from
classic to contemporary in
various media from wood and
metal to crystal*

Habitat
196 Tottenham Court Rd
London W1P 9LD
Tel. 020 7631 3880 and
0845 6010740 for
branches
customerrelations@habit
at.co.uk
Affordable stylish modern lighting

Heals
196 Tottenham Court Rd
London W1P 9LD
Tel. 020 7896 7555
Range of contemporary lighting

Christopher Hyde
180 Wandsworth Bridge
Road
London SW6 2UF
Tel. 020 7731 8830
sales@christopherhyde.
co.uk
*Classic chandeliers, uplights,
wall and table lamps*

Ikea UK
2 Drury Way
North Circular Road
London NW10 0TH
Tel. 020 8208 5600
*Wide range of modern and
traditional designs; stores
throughout the UK*

**Kensington Lighting
Company**
59 & 54 a-b Kensington
   Church Street
London W8 4HA
Tel. 020 7938 2405
Traditional and modern lighting

Jim Lawrence
Scotland Hall Farm
Stoke by Nayland
Colchester
Essex CO6 4QG
Tel. 01206 263459
www.jim-lawrence.co.uk
sales@jim-lawrence.co.uk
*Classic lanterns, pendants and
wall lights*

John Lewis Partnership
Oxford Street
London W1A 1EX
Tel. 020 7629 7711 and
020 7828 1000 for
branches
JL-oxford st@johnlewis.
co.uk
Classic and modern lighting

Liberty plc
Regent Street
London W1R 6AH
Tel. 020 7734 1234
*Traditional and contemporary
lighting*

Mr Light
275 Fulham Road
London SW10 9PZ
Tel. 020 7352 7525
*Contemporary and traditional
fittings*

Lipp
118a Holland Park
   Avenue
London W11 4UA
Tel. 020 7243 2432
Contemporary and classic lights

**London Lighting
Company**
135 Fulham Road
London SW3 6RT
Tel. 020 7589 3612
A wide range of modern lights

**Jeremy Lord
The Colour Light
Company**
Unit 28 Riverside
   Business Centre
Victoria Street
High Wycombe
Buckinghamshire
Tel. 01494 462112
Innovative colour installations

McCloud Lighting
3rd Floor Unit 19-20
Chelsea Harbour Design
   Centre
Lots Road
London SW10 0XE
Tel. 020 7352 1533
sales@mccloud.co.uk
*Hand-finished decorative
lighting*

Nice House
Italian Centre Courtyard
Ingram Street
Glasgow G1 1DN
Tel. 0141 533 7377
Unusual contemporary designs

Ochre
22 Howie Street
London SW11 4AS
Tel: 020 7223 8888
www.ochre.net
Stylish modern lamps

Porta Romana
West End Farm
Upper Froyle, Nr Alton
Hampshire GU34 4JR
Tel. 01420 23005
www.portaromana.co.uk
sales@portaromana
Range of contemporary lighting

Purves & Purves
80-81 Tottenham Court
   Road
London W1P 9HD
Tel. 020 7580 8223
European contemporary lighting

Renwick & Clarke
190 Ebury Street
London SW1W 8UP
Tel. 020 7730 8913
*Traditional wood, metal and
ceramic lights*

Roset UK Ltd
95 High Street
Great Missenden
Bucks HP16 0AL
Tel. 01494 865001
*Coordinated range of modern
designs and lighting for interiors*

SKK
34 Lexington Street
London W1R 3HR
Tel. 020 7434 4095
skk@easynet.co.uk
*Assortment of innovative
modern designs*

Space
214 Westbourne Grove
London W11 2RH
Tel. 020 7229 6533
*Contemporary interior design
with cutting-edge lighting*

Tindle Lighting
162 Wandsworth Bridge
   Road
London SW6 2UQ
Tel. 020 7384 1485
Antique and decorative lighting

Vaughan
G1 Chelsea Harbour
   Design Centre
Lots Road
London SW10 0XE
Tel. 020 7349 4600
www.vaughandesigns.
com
Stylish decorative lighting

Viaduct
1-10 Summers Street
London EC1R 5BD
Tel. 020 7278 8456
info@viaduct.co.uk
*Contemporary European
lighting*

Wilkinson plc
1 Grafton Street
London W1X 3LB
Tel. 020 7495 2477
Chandelier sales and repairs

Christopher Wray
600 Kings Road
London SW6 2YW
Tel. 020 7736 8434 for
branches
sales@christopherwray.
com
Traditional lighting designs

William Yeoward
Space S
The Old Imperial
   Laundry
71 Warriner Gardens
London SW11 4XW
Tel. 020 7498 4811
A selection of metal lamps

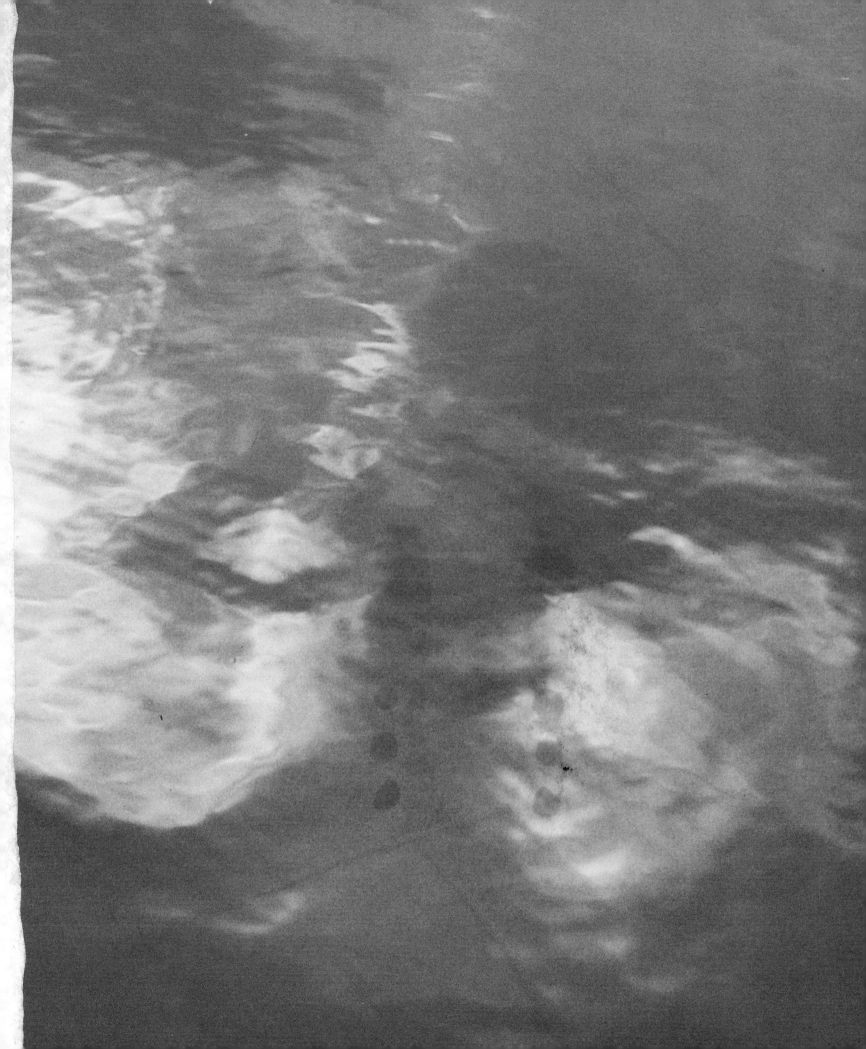